OWL OF THE MOON

Poems
by
Wing Williams

Each one of us a ripple

Which shall change the world

May we use this power wisely

Copyright © 2020 by David Kelly Williams who is Wing Williams.
All rights reserved. Other than brief passages or quotes in a newspaper, magazine, book in reference, radio, television review, internet review, or documentary, no part of OWL OF THE MOON may be reproduced in any form, through any mode, electronic or mechanical which includes recording or photocopying or any other type of information storage and retrieval system without written permission from the author Wing Williams (David Kelly Williams).

Manufactured in the United States of America

Williams, David Kelly
Williams, Wing

ISBN-13 978-0-9981127-3-2

TABLE of CONTENTS
Poems by
Wing Williams

Foreword	17
No More Walls	22
Midnight	23
Here with You	24
My Name	25
Never Dressed	27
The River Below	29
The Return – Part 2	30
Sharp Knife	31
The Snow	33
Bleeding	34
Choose Peace Once Again	35
March, In the Valley	37
Home	38
Waiting for The Wind	39
Sledding Hill	40
Mother's Wish	41
Young Coyote	42
Grandpa, McQueen & Me	43
A Humbling Moment	44
Morning Glimpse	45
Ghost in the Basement	46

The Darkness	47
Garden Gabbas	48
In Deepest Well	49
Suicide Waits	50
Two Wars	51
O'Malley	53
Toward Horizon Anew	55
The Maniac Above	56
Release of Day Upon the Night	57
Spring	58
As I Must	59
Each Heartbeat	60
Classical Kiss	61
Garlic	62
Midday on the Porch	63
Ourselves & Our Land	64
To the City	66
Is I	67
The Toad in Me	68
Hatchet	69
Time's Turns	70
Because of It	71
Till the Soul	72
Quiet Hours	74
Bathroom Poem	76
Day's End	77
Communicate	78
No More, Tonight	79
New	80

To Us	81
Dog-ish	82
Day Slid Away	83
Is It Worth It?	85
Ignore Them	86
My Very Own Fate	87
Soothe	88
Ambrosia	89
Hypocrisy	90
Dawn Piss	91
The Horror	92
Do You Hear Them?	93
Afternoon	94
Tucson Night	95
That Pre-Dawn Hour	96
Chaff of Disrespect	97
Trinity	98
Battle	99
Out of The Hole	100
Her Breath	101
The Barrio	102
Summer Decisions	104
Beyond	105
Another Wild Creature	106
Vision	107
Dead Tree?	108
Until	109
What We Destroy	110
The Bells	111

The Lady Slipper	112
This New Day	114
My Tired Lover	116
Take a Moment	117
Amber Rustle	118
Moon Thoughts	119
Breath of Time	121
Summer Clothes	123
This Lifelong Pursuit	125
Summer's Almost End	126
Dog by The Sea	127
Albatross	128
Melancholy Peace	129
The Violence We Never Met	130
Last Light	132
When We Could Smoke On the Patio	133
The Gnashed	135
Take Care of This Planet First	136
I Am an Owl Afterall	137
The Golden Hour	138
As if it Never Mattered	139
Shan't Stay Here Long	140
Let it Be & Then Remember	141
Midnight Words	142
9:39 PM	143
Eliminate	145
'til Well Past Noon	146
House Holding Shoulders Strong	147

Crossword at The Bar	149
Breath of Bread	150
Snowy Slumber After Sleep	151
Chaco and I	152
Insanely Me	154
Listen to Each Note	155
A New Way	156
Forgotten Leaves	157
Grazes, Retracts	158
Warm Winter Day into Night	159
Nirvanic Place	160
Keep Carrying Yourself	161
Feral Juice	162
Roan Highland's Croon	163
Here I Can Breathe	164
Lions and Ghosts	165
Sad Son	166
My Heart is in The Desert Tonight	167
A Father's Love	168
I Will Never Be Like You	170
The Transition	172
Puma Prowl	173
Yes I am	174
Dirty Days on The Farm	175
The Mirage is Ye	176
Maybe Blue	177
Anima Surge	179
We Are Not Bound	180
A Reminder	181

Dismal	182
Another Poem to The Moon	183
Pacific Crest Trail Morning	184
Between Asleep and Awake	186
Strike Me Again	188
Bellow	189
The Last Candle	190
So Quiet	191
Manta Ray	192
At Grandma's House	193
Om	196
Bird Parents	197
Babel Tower	199
Simply True	200
Exponentiate	201
Dripping Mustard B.C. (Before Covid)	202
Don't	204
The Power of You	205
Charleston to Savannah	206
Fatherly Beam	207
Tequila in a Cup	208
Lovers in Green	209
Upside Down	210
For Now	211
Why I Am Alive	212
Laze of The Land	214
These Suffocating Webs	216
Right About Now	218

"Trifles"	219
Like Seeds	221
Morning Reveille	222
Foxy	224
The Had-Enoughs	225
Arcane Layers	228
Cut the Ribbon	229
Reminder	231
Thoughts of Family	232
Not at the Cabin Yet	233
Oh Whirl-Wind Weapon of Wise	235
Awake at Night	236
Club of Maniac Porch Pacing Artists	238
Autumn	240
Tear on a Cheek	241
There I Must Go	243
Kill What Kills	244
Seed	245
The Gathering	246
Confined	247
I Suppose	248
It Is Time	249
Pertinent	250
Conspiring	251
Day of Sadness	253
Still Alive	254
Being Single Aint too Bad	255
Saved by a Drunken Friend	257
Our Only Time, A Memory	259

Rain's Remnants	262
True Balance	263
Living for We	264
Goddess Souls	265
Piano Grass	266
No More	267
Daily Heartbreak Routine	268
Unto New Lands	269
Anatomized	270
A Healthy Love	271
With a Limp	273
Jealousy	274
Haunt of Moody Night	275
How We Handle Today	276
A Dog's Digs	277
Common Bond	278
Carnally Divine	279
Murder Attempt	280
Concussed	281
Torment	282
A Reprieve	283
I Am Home	284
Purposeful Power	285
I Must Say	286
The Great Wave	287
Somewhere	288
So Very B.C.	289
Still Healing	290
Obliteration	291

In Bed	292
Change Shall Blow Thru	293
A Ripple	294
Anchor	295
Must Let Go	296
My Words	297
MAP	298
Cool Off	299
Infinite Treasure	300
Vault Within	301
Awake Again	302
Gracefully Forward	303
Battle of Brays	304
As I	305
Tempest	306
I and You	307
Ash of Once Was	308
A Call to Arms	309
St. Patrick's Day	311
Oh Darlin	312
Freshly Shaved	314
The Beginning	315
Coronavirus View	316
Heat of Time	317
This Too Shall Pass	318
An Unexpected Gift	319
You Are Strong	320
Persist	321
Dive into Possibility	322

Steadfast Beacons	323
I Dream of You	324
A New Me	325
I Am Only Human	326
Have I?	327
Vote	328
Bushwhack Thru	329
No Justice No Peace	330
I Fight for Us All	332
Umbrella in The Rain	333
A Few Moments to Pray	334
Labyrinth of Self	336
I Believe in You	337

For my faraway stellar friend

Lauren Eden

who too poured her anima
into poetry as she must

to heal, rise and conquer own self,
choosing beauty
within the dark

this book is for you,
thank you for always being you

and for reminding me
what D.H. Lawrence said

"I never saw a wild thing sorry for itself."

FOREWORD

I begin by thanking you for considering reading this book. I challenge you to do so, with intention of allowing the words and mystic meanings to penetrate deep into your soul. OWL OF THE MOON is no accident, as I am no accident, as you are no accident. This book is my third poetry book, the final installment of my first poetry trilogy.

> THE BEAR WITHIN
> AS A WOLF BREATHES
> OWL OF THE MOON

Nearly five years ago when I turned thirty years of age, I was in a place mentally and physically I did not want to be, not where I had planned, nor how I had envisioned turning the page on decades. The raucous twenties now but a yesterday and everyday more. My soul was in danger, psychological instability threatened to bury me beneath The Mariana Trench. Yet I knew, from knowledge I had gained through life, that this is where and how it must be. To try and drag the world backward, so as to never lose the sun of day, was wrong. To try and right the ship, by ignoring the holes in my hull would only lead to death. So, I sat in the rain next to a tree, with a glass of red wine in hand and a ribeye grilling behind, I closed my eyes, bathed in the tears that seeped out of my cracks and let the decade become. No longer would I live as I had, it was time for reinvention. It was time to take all those years of stories and lessons and put them down on paper, become what I had been preparing for, the writer I was born to be. Writing had always been a healing practice but never had I created a goal with such intention. In that moment, minute one of year thirty, I began to write THE BEAR WITHIN. The mission, three books of poetry within five years.

Book One was an intimidating task, as all three have been in unique ways, yet book one was, well, book ONE. Just as I had hiked the Appalachian Trail when I was twenty-four, the Pacific Crest Trail when I was twenty-six, among a myriad of new adventures, jobs and life trials each year, frightened yet determined I knew it all began with the first step, the first mile, the first mountain. It is simply a matter of doing, facing the unknown and stepping within.

One foot in front of the other, moving forward nothing less. Book One became exactly what I needed in my life. It allowed me to walk through the door and learn. It allowed me to see physical progress in the goal I had set. Full of mistakes, rough around the edges like myself, my rookie year if you will, accomplished.

Book Two AS A WOLF BREATHES was a whole new hinterland. Much like hiking the Pacific Crest after the Appalachian, I knew some of what to expect, but was also again entering an untrodden (to me) wilderness. Although The Bear was personal, written through the lens of mine own perspective, Book Two, The Wolf, dug deeper within as well as exposing more of who I am. I expected more of myself this time around, I needed to take what I had learned through my rookie year, apply and continue to mature within such. My own self, my own soul, my own art which reflects my depths, all must be stronger, more poignant, more exposing, challenging both me and you. No matter what it was to become I knew it would be raw and honest, and therefore what it must be.

Book Three, OWL OF THE MOON, took the longest of the three to write. It contains far more poems than my previous two. The first two books included a handful of prose style short stories, this one does not. This book spans the time of just over two years. During that era, I wrote over one-thousand poems, I give you nearly a third of those here. A little more than the first half of this book is focused on the joys of everyday life while battling heavy bouts of chronic depression. My dog my lover and I facing life together until heartbreak befell. The latter part of this book goes through the pain of being rejected by the one I had committed my heart to. (This too an important lesson I would grow from.) Shortly thereafter a murder attempt on my life disrupted my healing and a few months later I contracted the novel coronavirus; there are not many poems on those two topics for I was so physically incapable, I could barely write. OWL OF THE MOON finishes as I continue to evolve in all ways, body, mind and most importantly, soul.

In life there shall always be great hardships and trials, and though we do not wish for these to be, they are some of our greatest opportunities to flourish, for this I am grateful. If there was no pain how could we ever know joy?

I challenge you to perceive this book and all of my books through your own soul, let the words take you wherever that must be. My goal in baring who I am is to encourage you to find and be exactly who you must be. I believe in you and though we may never meet, I am grateful for who you are and your potential within. Focus on true agape love. Give this honestly to others and yourself, take one step forward and no matter the obstacle, keep on moving into the supreme unknown. May it be a marvelous pilgrimage.

Sincerely,

Wing Williams

NO MORE WALLS

After I finished my first long hike, the Appalachian Trail, my father met me at the base of Mt. Katahdin, the trail's northern terminus for a melancholic celebration. In Millinocket Maine we drank whiskey and beer, shot pool 'til ice froze, ate fish n chips, venison stew and blueberry pie, I made a speech, he beamed proudly at me. We bunked in the hostel, twin beds beneath one large window facing west, the mountains, my home. He fell asleep long before I could, upon a mattress, within walls.

At breakfast he sipped his coffee as I looked out the window. He drove me south-east, to the coast, to my truck and clothes, to my heap of nothingness. The miles whooshed by as radio opinions, with no regard to the slippery cold granite, to the red fox, to the hemlock. He left me there in my once was. After hugs and laughs and pictures of success, I sat alone and smoked a joint. Tears streamed down my face; I a bill being tucked back into the envelope of society. I knew what I must do, I knew who I had become.

MIDNIGHT

The night sky is clear save for the great
Migration of clouds, each its own, all a
Heard flying low, like the hero ghosts of
Eagles, or airplanes, or dust of goddess'
Dresses, or goddesses themselves each
Striking a pose and soaring at such an
Illustrious space above my tacit weight.
Are they flying to or away? Are they the
Heel or toe? Ominous peace, into bed I go.

4am

The dog whines at the door, a torrent of
Wind shudders the cottage, pinecones
And raindrops pummel upon roof as if
Heaven must be reckoned. Door opened
Peeing up into deluge, clouds of afore
Surely but pawns of war dragging the
Battering ram now seething. Dog shoots
Out into creaking grind of tempestuous
Cogs, barking at the sky and possible
Racoon. Lover listens to all, smiling warm
Between dreams and blankets.

HERE WITH YOU

In Autumn's last hour of daylight
Beneath blues parading silently away
Grasping tail of sun's southern draw

Where sagebrush scrapes denim knees
And footprints go where less are so
Humbly wrapped in sky's swaddle

Cheeks aflush with inspired grins
Badgers digging somewhere near
Steady breathes morph to laughter

Snakes slither subtly through shadows
Ardent ghosts whisper in winds
Emboldened from journey beyond

Our eyes wonderfully wide
Saturating in all this land's
Powerful magnificent beauty

Here with you
I hold your hand
And you hold mine

MY NAME

the train rumbles by again
piercing the silence of this early Tuesday
morn

screech of the rails
an irate chalkboard down the hall

monstrous horn blast
to each neighborhood it rolls past

all turning in sleep
as in nightmares not awake

belly bellow through town
tremors of sound
rippling ever closer
as it pales further away

all of five minutes rails wreak havoc
until the still is reclaimed

my heart beats exponentially beneath
stars enveloped in ebony

unfastened to the guidelines of our time
skin cloaked with bumps

as if the train has beckoned my name
whispers of dust never worn

NEVER DRESSED

Cherry tree silhouette,
balmy night skeleton black,
never dressed December,
no wedding in cold grasp
as winters past.

Rooftop pinnacles naked,
dedicated sentries dull
in slumber, lit oil lamp
in empty house -no mirage,
bears roll over agitated.

Gutters nailed to eaves
gurgle spring-like melodies,
water slips down poplar fingers
landing 'pon wind chimes
prattling this warm night.

"Ah rain oh rain,
lazy excuse for winters reign"
(thinks this mind of blink
within universe eternal
-elder to lifespan wink).

Is the petrichor evermore?
With sun higher on southern shore,

I smell the pulsating shift,
I hear the cries of northern drift,
I know the earth must repair
all damage we have incited here.

THE RIVER BELOW

My soul wore the shards of confusion
as a cactus wears its needles,
so, I lowered hand grasping forehead
and put it to the doorknob instead.

Out of asylum down the alley
west along grass tufted pebbled lane
cutting behind the hobbles
running faster cross the city's frame

until I reach the river below,
nestled beneath wise old trees
of winters hardened green
where purity remains untarnished.

Here, warming body flows
beyond the blues of claustrophobia
to mine own darkness's,
I must exhale the angst.

Here, as the water judges not
I disembogue each sorrow
until the tears and sweat
forge my soul with soil again.

THE RETURN – PART 2

The return we joked
For many a reason

Wild-tree-desert-children
Click-clackin down city streets

Brown shoes to dance in
Peppered lips to press
Glittering shimmers thru
Sweaty fingers to grasp
A stem, tumbler, pint-glass
Or you in photobooths
Where grins slip to cat-like purrs
And paisley walls
Turn into
Long street-lamp lines
Of vintage candlelight
Whispering lover's lullaby
Of tired piano's melody
Still meandering the rows
'til it reaches another wind

SHARP KNIFE

Pen and pencil
Fresh pocket notebook
Crisp corners soon to be bent
Dirty fingerprints pressed
Full fettered papers layered
In boot-box in proper order
In room that creaks
Above partial tiled kitchen

Moccasin silence
In song-storm thickets again
In eye-poke fluster
Needles leaves bones twigs
Nose-canals ear-caverns infiltrated
Stabbing gums tween teeth
Chewing as a panda

Hush of heartbeat settled
Pon yesteryear's decay
Crumbled brown bits
Crawling slithering ground
Notebook open to blank page
Audubon anima inspiration
Buzzing forest tangle of life

New birds new bugs
Sketched described

All observations recorded
Most important notes wear
Arrows connecting thoughts
The chickadee truly sings its name
The owl is not fully invisible
-pellets of bones by toes

Vivacious ants maraud chaotically
Though harmoniously up and over
Brittle barrages once glitter above
Deciduous clusters low
Conifer clumps high
Doe's wary eye never vexed
By beaver tail echo
Ripple to pond-lip's side sippers
Skeets skim surface skin

"The forest is an orchestra,
A family to which I belong"
-the fox agreed tacitly
Hunched astute listening in trees

In an apothecary of truth, I shall bathe everyday
Never to be washed by greed's destructive ways

Ardent letters arranged above
Observations of a red-tailed hawk

THE SNOW

A mystic sleep
Settling deep
Into bones of earthly structure

Chilled marrow of dormancy
Submitted peace
Halfway until crocodile's drink

Twisting
Into outer space without feeling
Until clouds dissipate

Lovers last tangle before train
Winds exhausted
As strewn bottles

Moon shining forgotten lust
Upon dance shoes with no feet
Silence

A beast with no shadow

BLEEDING

For a crack
Shall become a chasm
If not mended

Love the suture
Seams of communication
Bond sanctuaries together

Souls patiently focused
Upon heart of the other
To purely hear what is true

Igneous passion forging
Mountains of breathing rock
Likening other breath as one's own

Evolution united

Celestial rise of nirvanic emprise
Never to ripen
If but an island adrift

Tendrils taut no more

CHOOSE PEACE ONCE AGAIN

Midnight psychosis,
not quite.
Needle unhinged,
no true north,
illusioned dancing candlelight
disarmed heart attacked by succubus.

My gravity is stronger
than this I know,
spinning within
black hole,
untamed meddlesome miseries
resurrected from dormant graves.

This grip shall not
fully slip
but first
let me writhe ravenously,
for all in which I believe has
disappeared, as a tree in the fog.

Gray devouring thing,
toward beastly
jagged gnash
I wobble,
to slay invaders with truth,
exponential knowledge murky.

Each moment
I have existed
trekking thru both
darkness and light
has escorted me to now,
by own pace of pilgrimage.

Boldly I enter this door
and choose peace once again.

MARCH, IN THE VALLEY

Falcons perch on power lines
Farmers chat by tractors
In fields with silver green glow
Stretching bellies and throats
Each transfixed
Manifesting different crops
At different speeds
Fast as cars or slow as cigars
For mice are axels
Pigeons are pistons
Practice of knowledge represent

Patient earth slowly gulps
Drench of winter undress
Styling boots to knees
And beaks to plumage
Seeds are spread
As bird descends

Pursuit of sustenance
For another tomorrow

HOME

Waking up in darkness
my hand does not reach for you
for it is firmly grasped
by your hand.

Conversations in dreams
morph to roll of ocean waves
your breath bending the reeds
of my chest as breezes do.

You stir as my eyelids open,
as if simply silent shades
drawn before, connected
to your marvelous mind.

Tendrils of light travel thru
our fingers and gazes and
tongues of speech or silence
long enough to wrap the world,

ethereal vines we nourish
each day, lighthouse
upon a foundation
we have come to call home.

WAITING FOR THE WIND

His beard and sailboat both white
with streaks of dirty wisdoms
years of drips and evaporations
as veins of compressed epochs
layer the soil beneath feet.

In front of his boat
is his truck, fastened
four-wheel locomotive for this
tree-to-sea life,
clydesdalian patient steed
with reigns now slack
awaiting the captain's command.

A hut he built
stands fitted in the cab,
atop this abode a shingled roof
and a cat in the hut
poking out orange head
rubbing side of spine long
smoothly upon small open door,
by which he leans silently
this man of the sea older than I,

waiting for the wind
to push him again,
gray eyes to gray sky.

SLEDDING HILL

The snow dons a sheet of crusty ice.
Thick shelf for children to run upon,
until jumping and sinking to the waist.

The sledding hill has become
many half tunnels with crisp
crinkled fingers as ceilings,
miniature version of streets
slicing New Hampshire forests.

Just as fast too – we thought,
as feet first then head first
then standing style all tumbled
into the slap of crystal cold.

Skin cries no story of discomfort
for cold is simply a way to be.

Back to the top of the hill
and down again, until we feel
our bellies yearn and
imagine our mother's worry.

MOTHER'S WISH

"I wish
we could all live
in one big house,
or many little houses
all close together,"

my mother once said.

"All of my children
with their children,
a big garden, a big hearth…"

Words so far away,
ripple but glass to the eye.

YOUNG COYOTE

A young coyote
runs along my horse limping
until velvet shade
one tree amongst sage.

He stops to lick
red thigh dripping
then smile
thru summer-tired pant.

I look back and wonder
steering steed to turn and slow,

if indeed this young coyote,
will heal enough to fully grow.

GRANDPA, MCQUEEN & ME

If I was a car
I imagine myself
as a 1968 Mustang fastback
with Steve McQueen's ghost
as the pilot
lighting 2 cigarettes and a joint
at the same time
feeding me all the smoke I desire.

If I was a car
and Steve's ghost was driving
we'd torment the pavement
and go pick up my grandfather.
Down there in sticky summer Gainesville
he'd jump in and tell us
"roll up the windows,
tobacco only, none of that hippie shit."

But I'm not a car
and Grandpa is a spirit,
so, I suppose this'll never happen.

A HUMBLING MOMENT

Mother grizzly speaks abruptly

Stench of air her standing there.

Two cubs scatter behind and thru

Greens I dare not look into,

For all I see is her protective eyes

Slow motion knowledge of reality;

I've become the salamander

Who hopes drunk folks don't tread on me.

MORNING GLIMPSE

It was only a visit,
snow arrived at midnight
then rushed off rooftops
before breakfast, like a squatter
with a charming smile, saying
"you already know me
so why get to know me again?"

Tomato youths broke the soil
in warm window boxes at first light,
a babe is to be born -then 1,000 more,
generation of love in our hands
to nourish and provide fenceless fields
of endless evolution beyond today.

Bare skin wears melanin dances
lips lick sunbeam kisses between
body-rotations north-south,

rotisserie celestial travelers we are
rising passionate souls of a star.

GHOST IN THE BASEMENT

I bend over
To transfer
The wet washed load of laundry
To the dryer
Swipe filter of lint
Toss soft gray into trash
Focus on efficient movements

A cold finger swipes my neck
Sharp nail long scrapes skin

No one is here but me, I know

Basement door still open
The dog whines without entering
Not a mouse has housed
This one blue-chaired cellar

There is no one here, whom I know

THE DARKNESS

Oh, so heavy
lays this blanket
suffocating me
tearing me
drowning me
pulling me deeper
apart
from all light
from all understood vibrations
to shrieks of demonic
underground heat which yields
no breath of relief;

although I remember,
upon this sand-throated descent,

I have learned to swallow
the entire universe,
always to rise again.

GARDEN GABBAS

Beneath a waning gibbous
We smoked the gabbas
Cats and boots in midnight sway
Fire cackling a savage way
Dog mimics black panther
Curled in orange chair
Her eyes aglow
Color of -I see you-
Our garden beds
Now on edge of darkness
Lay still only half tilled
Not like a sheep run away
Half sheered with buttocks shivering
Or that tiny jerk of a horse in Wyoming
Or even my day-time dreams
But as if
A vigorous mole took a nap

IN DEEPEST WELL

Once I stopped believing in hiccups
they never returned.

Once I ceased swatting mosquitos
and fearing wasp mingles
slowing to discuss, exchanging
perspectives and appreciations,
new respect birthed peace.

No bug shall disturb me, only I can do that.

Tho the snake slithers close
it shall not bite,

As bears in the fog begin to nod
when tacit tones wear kindness;

for dimensions are decisions
and language an ethereal thing,
we only use words
to try and translate this.

Further within,
in deepest well
described as soul,
only there can we create
all opportunities untold.

SUICIDE WAITS

With tingle of Still Alive Peace
I charged through March fog into an
orange eyelash sleepy dream.

Train tracks nearly home
turtling across PaClunks, mist,
distant light, snow death breath,
I knew I must stop and capture this.

Down the corridor I nimbled,
Nikon D200 in hand,
200 feet from the road
seemed enough to not disturb possibility.

As I was laying upon belly within
parallel tracks twixt skeletal oaks,
I heard their snow crunches,
jingle, scoff, two cops creeping up on me.

"Are you tryna commit suicide?!"
"Are you waiting for the train?"

I turned head and shot them both

nah, I showed them the photo.

TWO WARS

One difference between depression and
anxiety
is the grip each holds.
Thru heavy murk of depression
I can create art that mollifies
quicksand angst of purgatory.
During heavy bouts of anxiety
I can do nothing.

Wrapped too tightly to breathe unable to
exhale
mind-storm within a soul ground beneath
a millstone taller than Babel ever reached,

and yet, I am no longer paralyzed,
for with anxiety, I have learned
it is a battle I shall always overcome
and depression
simply a war-cloak I calmly wear
as a comrade who darkly reminds
the true shine of my light.

And so, as anxiety goes,
I writhe and panic,
hermit and grin
knowing I am the one who wins,
and when appeased to depression

with emancipated sigh,
I create and love and raise my chin -forever.

Never tomorrow, always today,
turning tomorrows
into today.

O'MALLEY

"I've been doing this for over 50 years."

My coffee tasted like maybe halibut shit.

"Never another life for me," he spat.

Obviously. Old man with orange legs
salted brow and three ex-wives
who left him smiling at lobsters.

"You ever love any of them?"
I ask, "the wives I mean,"
dodging bumps of morning blue jumps,
the sea a trampoline for fastened green
knees.

"Not enough," he muttered,
slowing down the grind to a lull and
sunrise bigger than his belly.

O'Malley pulled out an alligator flask
and smirked, nose-tinge-pour
into coffee each,
he a nemesis of crustaceans,
and women, it seemed.

"Kid this might not be the job for you,

so, fuck you and cheers!
Today we gather lobsters,
tomorrow you find another boat
or go climb the mountains."

And so, it became,
with a solid handshake
and different names.

TOWARD HORIZON ANEW

Running with intention
and inspiration towards
horizon I shall reach.

Striving upwind
or flying fast
upon wings

until silent still
that never remains
is replaced by knowledge

and emboldened zeal.
I charge again
toward horizon anew

diving further
into each evolved
beautiful unknown.

THE MANIAC ABOVE

Here comes another squall!

Newborn buds shivering thru it all
tremors of cold raucous pockets
dart about pimpled volcano land
spitting hail upon chins warm to the sun.

Like an alarm clock shriek
right after slipping back into sleep
no true peace with sure to come beeps
tho as sure as snooze silences hail
another deca-repose bathing in stills,

the maniac above shall return.

RELEASE OF DAY
UPON THE NIGHT

When she sleeps
and I cannot

When the moon
has tied a knot

To my brain's
wild wolf like ways

Turning dreams
into mystical haze

Luring soul within the cold
to howl with winds eternally old

I step outside to bathe
beneath icy skeletal waves

Lifting chin to the moon
my chest ungripped

To daylight's tune

SPRING

Daffodils tween volcano hills

Hum xanthous petal melodic trills

Lifting corona trumpets to the sun

A trillion instruments sing along

We each one part of Mother's song

We each a note of the earth

Together an orchestra

Of budding mirth

AS I MUST

Writing is my breath
without it I will die,
for I was not placed
upon this planet to be silent.

If I am, if I do not
shout my existence in stride
to declare beauty, to destroy injustice,
to embolden evolution of love,
to save the children from slavery
to illuminate all that is good
to tell stories of now so that tomorrow
we can continue to progress,
to pour my soul upon
mountains of ever-changing fortitude,
if I do not, if I am silent,
then I will have wasted every smile
you all ever gave me, each leaf
turning in a breeze, every molecule
of who I am, my heart-yearns
of unfathomable depth.

If I do not write and too
call for your attention,
I shall fade as chaff and no more.

EACH HEARTBEAT

Writing poetry is often simply
describing what I think
in the way that I think it.
No twist of fancy,
it is impossible to invent new colors
one must learn to seem them, to feel them.
For it is true, that lady there, her demeanor
is that of a misplaced queen
born into an invisible world (to me);
or the sun only a fraction as warm
as my lover's loving kiss,
or the spring flowers the budding tears
of a creator's heart
slashed by a monster only met in mirrors.
I think, I write, I see
the father leaning in for a hug
yet the son pulling back for a handshake.
I listen to the whisper of a shrug,
to the melody of trash bins
dragged and dumped
by a relieved whistling now tipsy cook.
I smell the Juniper burn, differently,
January or August, I regurgitate
each heartbeat, buried no more,
set to fire, burned to stars, on wing set free.

CLASSICAL KISS

We kissed to Debussy

Slowly at first

but then

Each note danced more zealously

Pulsing passion reached unfathomed speeds

Heavenly seeds helicoptered around

Twitter-pated day swirled upside-down

Nothing recognized
but melting blurred cognizance

Of this crescendo-ing
enveloping
worshipping
finger-toe earth digging

Classical kiss.

GARLIC

She suggested shrimp pasta
with that butter cheese parsley prim,
considering all items
our fridge held within,
and as our excitement
rose with the moon
so continued pink romp
of drinks-afternoon.
Dancing on dirt discarding all socks
'til we fell on the ground
and laughed away clocks.
Cherry pits sticking
to wild sun-licked hair
neighbor dogs responding
to howls in the air.
Eyelashes rest too satisfied for blinks
dirt travels on shoulders
to bedroom sheets.
Oh, a day away
from all rules that delay
any childlike cooing
at what clouds have to say
is forever the place
we go when we love.
And now, with an owl's hoot
and warm thankful hands,
I dice garlic.

MIDDAY ON THE PORCH

Dog bark

Distant hyenic laughter

Woman yips like she likes it

Car screeches

Horn for horn howl for holler

Bird killed by bigger bird

It only sounded like murder

OURSELVES & OUR LAND

Into the soil digging with my hands
befriending earthworms
feeling mother heartbeat.

My knees as nose fingers as tongue
remembering why I was born and
childish truths, for mud truly does
taste like cookies.

Got a 4-row corn patch
tilled and sown in noon sun,
sneezing dirt back to dirt
like the worm
I am part of the earth.

Tomatoes and marijuana ever stronger
in greenhouse constructed artfully,
upside down table,
Prairie Wagon – we kid,
our own Oregon Trail
blazed with necks getting red.

Ah hee! Bring on the heat
with the rain that makes atmosphere hazy
in a sun undone from winter's long reign.

The flowers are reaching

the radishes are quaking
all the land is breathing
with seeds germinating

hearts sprouted once again
as we use what we have
to love ourselves and our land.

TO THE CITY

A city boy
I'll never be

tho I'll visit
only to see

if mountain words
can ring a bell

with all the yearns
your souls do yell.

IS I

The throb of a mountain beast
Is he
Shaking in knees born to be free
Of shackles like roads
Or limits like loads of
Everything he's told
To be.
Can you smell the petrichor?
The scent of earth
On heaven's door,
The very thing you begin to be
Whence forfeiting laws
Of society's breed.

THE TOAD IN ME

Disapproving the practice of past
the toad declined
the hopping contest.

He felt if he lost,
then maybe he'd feel categorized,
and if he won, well then
when they pat his head
how could he believe them?

And so, the toad left them all
to find a pond
no other toad had ever swum.

HATCHET

Splinters and cuts carved
youth into adulthood

Wood-grain stories remain
after splits and smoke
smear sanity like warm butter
smoothly
across cheekbone of soul.

Past remorse naked
for heads do not hang
when smoke seeps
between dirt and skin,

alive within alien corpse
thinking maybe we belong
then deciding we do,

Mother Earth
settling disputes
within iron fist of time,

we digging fingers
beyond dirt.

TIME'S TURNS

Things don't always go

The way we want them to

Thank goodness

For if they had

I would not be here

In love today

With you

BECAUSE OF IT

The verdant hues of spring
Have waned
Into a tawny slow breathing
Palomino

The sun of today but
A mound
Of cold desert dripped
Candle wax

The violin she played as
Dusk departed
Now trembles alone
In her case

And I
And you
Are who we are
Because of it

TILL THE SOUL

We need to change the way
we speak to people.
Young people for instance,
they don't respond to boxes,
they will burst out one way or another,
positively or negatively.

Mental illness is what we define
as not the standard,
creating more boxes.

Not all minds are yours,
in fact, each is different.

When I was young and rebellious
I responded positively to patience
and wisdom of knowing they didn't know.

To sail into mists together I could accept,
to be ruddered as livestock,
all fences will be destroyed.

We need to slow down
and not determine what is best for another.

Till the soil,
till society's soul,

create an environment
which produces health
not hypocrisy.

QUIET HOURS

The neighbor walked over to me
in pajamas, angry and stern yet
quite quiet about it all,
as if he'd be worse than I,
to proclaim his room is there,
at end of pointed finger.

"I know" I say,
wondering what wrong
I might have committed this time.

"You cannot bang on the drum!"
-he hissed,
my fingers grazing ancestral holiness.

"You cannot make noise!"
-everyone shouts
drowning me down
to no good numbed out.

No drums
No howls
No music
No dancing
No bothers
No questions
No mystery

No wild
NO ME!

"It is too late at night to sing!"
-they all yell at me.

BATHROOM POEM

When cleaning own bathroom
it is best to commit,
strip off all clothes
and truly dive in,
stretch to the corners
sniping all fuzz
slide upon porcelain
forfeiting sludge,
for everything in here
I once maybe was
and once it shines clean,

I'll wash me next.

DAY'S END

It seems irreverent
to not slow to a stand
and gaze upon the land
with each day's end.
(A sit with a smoke and a drink,
all the better.)

If for just one humble second,
soul aroused allowing completeness
bathing
in the royal subtle sigh of transition

birdsong bleeding peaceful blessings

holiness of her turn awake, asleep,
silent sheet drapes her naked body,

coyotes yip in evening mists

quiver sensed within fingertips

winds change directions
as breaths barter with eternity.

COMMUNICATE

When we argue
Squabble
Communicate not enough

I nearly drown
Gasping for the air
Of your heart

But then
You pull me up
Away from darkness

We emotionally spill
Remember
All that is true

Then sail
Stronger together
Always again

NO MORE, TONIGHT

I hear teethpaste sashaying

smell rosemary upon
finest of all things,

lights eliminate as footsteps
scurry to silent position,

-only the fluff of pillows-

I must go inside

and write no more poetry,
tonight.

She is waiting.

NEW

A new kind of joy

Never known
Until patience

Life lived

'til moons
Argued pink or purple
Humbled to the
Knowledge of time

Love now is a flower
That had yet
To exist

TO US

You drip over me
Like candle wax

Each breath
A suture
Saturating
Caressing
Strengthening bones

Petrichor skin
Encompassing soul

I have become
A part of your own.

(to her, to earth, to me)

DOG-ISH

Curled packed tight
Yet never asleep

Round black-boa wolf-leopard thing

Double chocolate donut
Snug to leg by fire
In stars greatest gleam

Tho first to wake always it seems

As kangaroo does
Two paws with claws
In humanish hang

Standing staring eyes glaring
At every bird and squirrel awake

Night to morning in the woods

DAY SLID AWAY

The wind has dissolved
Night has arrived

A day slid away
Is exactly what it is

Tones of let-go jazz and
Sleepy colors exchange

No more bills
No more business

Only silky sighs
Of content existence

~

I lay in awe
As you softly drift into sleep

I think of
All those days on mountains alone

When I yearned for this
Sunset seeking unknown tacit approval

Emotion erupting

Only in spaces no one will ever see
Until you

IS IT WORTH IT?

Sometimes I wonder
if what I'm doing
will ever even matter,
what is this even worth?

For the earth shall repair itself,
one day rid all parasites,
burn and freeze
detox anew, and yet

I somehow know
the stories we tell,
memories of old
lessons of yore,

the way we behave
right now, in this moment,
will become
the mold of so much more.

There are places we shall go
none of us yet know,
and so,
I shall keep believing.

IGNORE THEM

He has a tortured soul,
they all seem to say,

the wanderer of the fold
the black sheep gone astray.

He's never gonna make it,
old ones munching hay

the same shit they'd been eating
since they all obeyed first day.

MY VERY OWN FATE

Sliver of moon in clear night sky

Avenue of stars between tree tops

Floating alone in canoe down river

Dangling toes skimming dark water

Leaning back with earth my lover

I just a part of all of the others

Embracing the fact, I can create

All of my dreams, my very own fate

SOOTHE

The sky tonight
is licking the skin on my face

Shedding the dust of yester
seducing my eyes in Venus' shine

As 10,000 howls
sing the lines of summer

As soft string guitars serenade

As blues marry pinks
swaddling eastern underbelly

Clouds of grace laced
siphoning breaths thru trees
'til heaven's nest is reached

The sky tonight sets my soul free

The sky tonight soothes all of me

AMBROSIA

This
is pristine poetry music.

The groaning silent mountain monster
breath,
the incessant frog party,
the laughing wind ghosts
whispering wonderful secrets,
sniff and crunches never seen,
crisp orchestra of ethereal
and tangible with no glossy glare.

This
is the bear and the wolf
and the owl of the moon.

HYPOCRISY

In the woods
are the witches,

Whom have been said
will turn you wicked,

"Souls that do not believe
in civic-rules of today."

Savage Saints, some may spit
if being drunkenly honestly lit,

But even then, they walk home,
away from the woods

Away from whence they come.

DAWN PISS

Barely dawn, eyes cannot.

Why would they now? The dream,
your breath, cavern of warmth…

but I cannot fight
half-sleep discomfort any longer,

I unzip - I trip -the tent - naked
to urinate amongst sharp biting

cold of mountain morn.
Warm stream swallows crystals like lava.

I empty my sleep disturbance
into place all wild creatures do,

then back into cavern I fall
…your breath, our nook of sleep.

THE HORROR

Full fan tail of white

Brown giant down

Descending upon crown

Of shadow saturated

Vermin no more.

But as the wings loft

Victoriously

To feast another day,

Grounded mother

Screams her curses.

DO YOU HEAR THEM?

It has been some time since I said,
"do you hear the whispers slithering?"

For adults have funny boxes
they can't seem to see out of.

I still jump into rooms
expecting to trap the voice,

transfixed by matter just a mist
all brain is dust in compacted twist.

It has been some time since I said,
"there are no monsters beneath my bed,"

for now, I believe many things,
a child discerns without doubt.

AFTERNOON

Sitting in the dirt,

watching the wind badger pine needles
'til trillions of eyes open the sky
and memories amass in celestial tune,

family and pilgrimage,

falling back upon earth elongated,
gratefulness and savagery overtaking,
laughing rich wildly cognizant howls

daring the underside of everything

knowing
that nothing will tarnish this soul
for everything is never known.

TUCSON NIGHT

The train rolls by
every hour
or maybe more – I'm not sure

for the heat has a way
of slowing things down…
but sounds, like colors and smells

they are another tone
sharply boldly pronouncing existence
as if heat rising is not alone

mystery shedding many truths,
cacti green against blue
missions still impression-ed

thru barrio and presidio.
100 days without rain
but when it came all mouths

opened to the sky, and now,
as reds and clays rest
with teals and bricks,

night wears a silky sigh.

THAT PRE-DAWN HOUR

At 4:20 am the birds begin their song,
just one then two until many participate,

sweeping away stars, cheering on the sun,
dark blues forgetting all black undone

slid away like a tissue in a park
in a breeze when no one looks,

dawn's arrival set for display
ancient moments now west resting

with day as nocturnes slipped,
but that is neither here nor east

no one trying to catch up or slow down
just letting now be now,

as the birds do, as the sun comes,
as we celebrate a new today.

CHAFF OF DISRESPECT

"She is more to be pitied
then censored," he sang,

the world assuming
an imbalance of respect,

(for man must have sequestered
the only dignity she didn't lack).

NO woman should ever be censored
as honor should never be trashed

as ghostly notes still carry on
as history's howls sing its song

so that the future
will no longer tolerate inequality.

Thank you, mother and every other,
thank you, lover and every woman,

you embolden myself and
the world to destroy

draconian chaff
of disrespect.

TRINITY

The soul knows
what the brain doesn't

yet the brain can be trained
to tell the body

how to move with the soul,
listening to each other,

a symbiotic trinity
finely tuned to fly.

BATTLE

Hunger

Exhaustion

Insomnia

Depression

Paranoia

Delirium

Vertigo,

You shall not win.

OUT OF THE HOLE

It is very much

Like living in a dark cave,

Absorbing very little light

Then suddenly emerging

To the slap! Pupil's dilating,

Sheer sonic bright defecating peace

Of what one is accustomed to.

HER BREATH

Laying on the patio
summer's warmth wearing
night's northern sweater,

shooting star only seen
between a kiss or thoughts,
garden verdantly asleep

donning ebony purples with
sleepy droopy sighs.
Angel at rest

her head upon my chest,
her breath the metronome
of my attention.

THE BARRIO

It became one of those vacations the soul truly needed without first knowing.

No beach, no pomp, much circumstance.

A vacation where everything is just enough different another side of the brain is awoken.

The heat swaddled as coconut oil was carefully not spilled, only dipped and rubbed where sweat ceased to exist if water was drunk too shyly.

Another town in motion a little slower, different colors, margaritas beneath shade and mists-made, evening walks growing more vigorous as southern sun set.

In sticky dreams I can hear the jaguar scream, or perhaps the nearby cries of children and family separated by uniforms I observed at lunch.

Drip of forehead into nirvanic sandwich, hot grease on chin cooling me down.

At home water is a duty, here, ice is
pursued and water a delectable treat.

From ours to another, toys in corners,
pianos in rooms never forgotten only
amassed, children running into each other
intentionally and not, as dogs bark at noises
like cats turn away.

Cacti is the forest, lizards are the ground,
rattlesnakes seem to stake all the desert
outside town.

Boarded down once-was' linger like
cockroaches laying upside down, frantically
writhing until the final nail covers the
window for good.

The air is honest, most smiles are honest,
this reminding me of much more.

Walking the streets of the barrio, hole in
straw hat creating head top dust patch, I
rise my head with the saguaros and smile a
brutal grin to the sun.

SUMMER DECISIONS

Summer summons seizing of days
beginning with the cooler morn,
birds escort the familiar smell
of an earthly stew simmering soon,
heat rises, duties molassify.

One soldier of tyranny unlocks the door
forfeiting injustice for morality,
children must be with family, he knows,
so, he does what is right
not what he's told.

BEYOND

The city beats my brain like a box

Stomped to be flattened and tossed

Unapproved violent shattering

Shakes mindful carbonation

Murmur of devils on the loose

Bloodshot glares from eyes of spies

Slithering thru the empty space

A ribbon route I must decide

Until I've reached the holy place

Of silence beyond downtown's line

ANOTHER WILD CREATURE

Crossing the street a previous eve

a rambling raccoon and I
found ourselves alone
beneath warm waning moon,
other humans no closer than indoors,
just the trees and we, paces away,
asphalt beneath our 6 feet,

upon dance hall which
we did not dance upon

only peered fondly
slowly
closely
upon the other,

each peacefully pleased
to see another wild creature.

VISION

Wavering wisps of periphery
project thoughts into memory

Of perhaps past lives, or perhaps
superpowers of personification

Away from expectations,
alive adrift thirstily savagely

Exponentially free.

DEAD TREE?

They call it a dead tree
But it doesn't feel that way
Horizontal upon the ground
Old man never buried

Disintegrating yet still listening
Fungi growing like barnacles
Upon his back in his armpits
I standing upon sunken lungs

His breath tickles my feet
Causing laughter and joy
Which beckons the world to dance
Mitigating fear into peace

If there is no soul in you
Then there is no soul in me
Body may gift itself for another
But your spirit shall always be

UNTIL

In the dark
on the dirt
I string words together.

Settled in with spider dens
back pillow a tree trunk
turpentine floor

dog growling at
potential possibility

alley fight
not tonight

smirking chewing
ponderosa cambium.

I scribble
a whole buncha nonsense,

until I reach the poem.

WHAT WE DESTROY

I can feel it, even see it,
the invisible now apparent.

Cyclone fist punch of glory

dead trees and once living beings,
all souls summoned
resurrections redirecting seethe

as Hades prepares,
apparition army invades to reclaim,

wind thrusts fierce orange flak
embers all directions, black
clouds of mortal end envelop

tremors disengage earth-mass
swallowing stench of modern sins,
tsunamis rage forth intentionally

holy pimples vomit molten blood to
scab upon withering saddened cheeks,

for with her anger she shall do
all she must,

to repair what we destroy.

THE BELLS

The Bells tolled its noon day tell
reminding everyone they were there
and we are here, somewhere,

deciding breakfast or deciding lunch,
unleashing suits with smoothies
and dog naps in this heat,

Why suits?
I'd take a knife to mine
if somehow, I'd become a suit.

Would I even carry a knife then?
I wonder, for maybe I'd have already
forgotten
or been misled,

Stockholm Syndromed into not
slicing my suit at the knees
shoulders
neck, let me breathe!
Nay, no suit for me.

The moon and I travel
the world at night,
I'll take my breakfast
with the bells instead.

THE LADY SLIPPER

I came upon a Lady Slipper in the woods,
tucked tween lush ferns upon a hummock
overlooking verdurous marsh, lilies and
cattails
'til two beavers swam free dragging trees
gleaming yellow teeth, but she, this flower
was pink like a fairy tale asleep.

I sat next to the little queen, ever
so tender, careful not to disturb her;
a gentle curtsy she gave me, the same
way elephant eyes shine after crying,
So, I laid closer, upon belly full of berries
and settled my nose as close as the bee's.

She hummed painting the air invisibly
oculizing mystery into molecules,
she whispered to the beavers
whom did not listen, but the deer did,
and now a doe stood above our heads
swaddling sweet breath upon we.

Her muzzle likened my mother's touch
to which the orchid did not shun
for bravery is an important trait
when you're the only one.
Our biscuit buff sniffed kindly to say

"I will not pluck this queen today."

Quiet in the green, plump pastel slipper
lifting only one velvet eye slowly,
doe reposed in soft ferns, beaver slaps
warning others, the forest cast
a thousand sun-dials, and so the day
did go, drifting into verdant dreams.

THIS NEW DAY

Within peripheral – I see them,
looming
lurking
crunching dead leaves irregularly
monstrous scrape
claw drape
invisible bender of space
earthen shapeshifters
decimating shadows of morality
the minions of insanity
wearing capes darker than night
vying for soul only a fiber apart
from drowning to depths unfathomable.

Scent of wind I know I've met before,
ominous wolf guardian admonishing,
indigenous glimmer imparting wisdom
a mortal truth bred before fire,
forest funneling scripture
thru this skin I wear
with witchy haunting breathes into
carnelian chasms,

as a monk prays without knowing,
ceasing never yet simply being,
I listen.
As a flower raises head,

I hear.
Go home to the neverland minions,
graven cracking heart no more,
wounds to scab and scar,
my failures to not be a waste
yet the rubble of past,
soil of diamond compression
paving way for the intention
and refocus of this new day.

MY TIRED LOVER

She wore the limit of today
within her expression, brow
lowered gently, fingers grasping
as raspberries rest after harvest.

She spoke revving the engine
burning last fuel, how many
words are even left, scattered
after the sun set yesterday;

She let her sighs release her
as warmth in a suture tends
a silk for denim, skin for silk,
freedom with sleep released.

TAKE A MOMENT

Listen to the thunder
growling by
a layer further
than the pigeon

Cooing over head
in the clamor
that is a million
green leaves

Bees pollinate
buzzing tween flowers,
dirt of the earth
sticks to my skin

AMBER RUSTLE

When Grandpa died,
there was much to be done.

Fix the door squeak,
build a fence,
gather the leaves then burn them,
silence while watching, except for beer gulp
and the amber rustle of time turning.

Roses need tending
as spring sets in.

He left his woodshop as if
I'd relearn again.

Forever an age, 10 or now,
sunglasses slightly bent
tool-chest behind tool-chest
patterns of perhaps now simply
brown wrinkled paper
smeared in ashes from
a Georgia day the sky fell.

Pecans
Rain
Music,
Coyotes yip in mist.

MOON THOUGHTS

Last week we wore nothing at home.
Unlock door run thru kitchen bedroom
tackle
rip clothes off, long slow meditative sigh,
fan flow satisfied,
naked.
Damn it was hot.

And then suddenly leaves crinkled
into crisp cooler morns, sap rising eves.
We pull on sweaters and fluffy socks
wrap blanket tight to watch
The Sturgeon Moon
this horripilated night.

~

As the moon ascends to its apex,
that almost full,
that almost come,
all trees shiver violently.
I hang my hammock
trusting the silver infinity
-and glide thru a time
I've only dreamed of,
like the things we believe we could believe
if all rules were abolished.

~

Upon a butte, listening to a train,
knives and oil and brutality.
Why? The moon is not so unkind
as to reminisce of such. But the land,
as natives say before they are slaughtered,
"perhaps we should not trust them,
perhaps, we should rise higher and destroy
this infection before it kills us all."

~

So many times, I've watched you,
from winter valley in cold still survival
your breath midnight's illumination
swallowing darkness's beneath
ridges nude
'til wind howls summer's tune,
pummeling again each
equinox-al turn with those nocturnal
peripheral freedoms as
Herculean stallion released
from blindness, as an eagle sees.

Full-moon-shine I feel you as I sleep,
owl-eye whom never winks, tonight,
until tomorrow when you slowly
melt away into another new.

BREATH OF TIME

Walking down street in mist,
no – fog, nay – smoke.

It smells as if
everyone is warming
by cackling fireplaces,
faces half in shadow
-petroglyph walls,
skin beneath blankets
-no clothes at all;

and yet the night
holds no cheer
of smokestack ascension
climbing to stars,
or crisp icicle taste
of air warranting warmth,

it feels in fact – unkind,
like I am wrapped and whispered
by conniving alien minds
crawling thru trees
without disturbing a leaf,
slithering into windows
'neath paint chipped eaves,
an ominous tone from ever so far
sucking 'never to me'

from mind's repertoire.

For maybe,
as a finger grazes my ankles,
maybe
this is the last walk I shall ever take
in this body I know as what walk I know,
maybe all this smoke
is the breath of time
and only I can see it on this silent night.

And so, my anxious pace
slows to a halt,
I bathe in mystery,
close my eyes
to the sheer darkness of everything
as if I've never seen before,
and then
after disassembling mine own molecules
to the fusion of time,

I open eyes again,
Emboldened,
reborn.

SUMMER CLOTHES

Summer clothes – torridly stained
tatters nearly – holding barely
rips from earth grips
dirt bruises – imprisoned in fabrics,
white – not quite,
hems humbled to ever stretching
loving rolling grit of life.

Sundays best became a joke
once I became a Huckleberry bloke,
gopher holes – green goose shits
denim frills dandruffing bits,
savagely soiled – seeking no answer
as mountain slashes silently scream.

Never fallen off a mountain
yet fallen down many,
this hat I wear was always there
all my stories in disrepair
accidently naturally styled,
quadriceps gray ashen smooth
rib cage soot by afternoon
wine-bid will return to dance
once summer drench wears no more pants.

"Sir, would you like a napkin?"
"Thank you, no, I've got a shirt."

"Babe, you should take the napkin,"
My lover purrs with a smirk.

THIS LIFELONG PURSUIT

The artistic practice is all consuming.
On one hand it liberates the soul,
elevates the mind to a place
where ethereal becomes tangible.

Art allows the truth of oneself
to flow symbiotically with the
unbound energy of existence.
And yet, on the other hand

it can become deeply terrifying,
for one must face the mystery
head on, directly, internally without
timidity, bathing in weight
of what must be told
searching for and communing
within mind's darkest caves.

The responsibilities I feel wear
shackles only released once I have
conquered this lifelong Herculean duty.

I have not yet conquered my calling,
within each step
I discover more I must do.

SUMMER'S ALMOST END

There was a breeze,
but it traveled on,
leaving leaves to hang
like dead bats.
The smoke was slithering,
now it sleeps,
heavy as fleece
upon summer feet.

Wildfire cackle
I almost hear,
rattlesnake's fear
suffocating,
imagining waves
of dry and wet
Kamaishi destruction
or Mendo tears.

A glass of wine extra,
piano keys sigh,
lover in bed
has now shut her eyes.

DOG BY THE SEA

Sand on snout is not the same
as lava land of ponderosa duff,

Japanese trees gargle pebbles
slipping as paws seemed to drift

Transfixed upon earthen yo-yo,
CRASH white fangs of azure beast

Tilting head and jumping back,
SMASH the wake of moon's big rake

Tongue hanging out in blissful laugh.

ALBATROSS

Blue to black
Sky to earth
Albatross glide from keyhole arch

Galleon keel
Starboard lean
Albatross warns of continental end

Thunder slap
Ocean gnash
Albatross unnerved pon wide wing spread

Lighthouse twirl
Emboldened edge
Albatross apparition on mist veiled ledge

MELANCHOLY PEACE

Sky painting seducing, ever-changing
me as you are you,

Wisps of watercolor haze draining
into trees of falling leaves

Never below only all of me
as the sap is blood and I am you.

A morphing woozy clarity,
a mourning peaceful everything.

THE VIOLENCE WE NEVER MET

Across the ocean it was happening
But we didn't know
arms tangled together

Toes settled into jumping falling
sand specks
Backs upon driftwood aged
beyond our age

Tectonic shift
plasmid undulation,
Granular crust
burrow lounge bash

Waves crashing in autumnal night
Like rams battling
like shattered journeys

Signals
ripples of morning muddled
pandemonium
of souls leaving bodies early

They across vast expanse
their cries

The ram battle of ocean
beyond soiled feet

Water is rising
land is melting
liquefying
swallowing structures
and all trapped within

We sit silently
shivering slightly tho warm enough
humbled, awed
harkening each violent wave

LAST LIGHT

Last light of day I see you
settling low upon the earth as I,
like the saunter of a hungry sloth,
or slip of generational dreams.

Last light of day you are barely
sliver of tangerine, now less,
gasping softly, humbly whispering
of night's seductive dress.

Last light of day,
first stroke of night,
I transform imbued,

all of me
both of you.

WHEN WE COULD SMOKE ON THE PATIO

Met up with the guys for some beer,
another Friday evening much like others
except now the night rolls in
sooner than before
when we wore shorts and little more.

"I'll see you at the saloon" we affirm,
each one of three coming in his own way,
the same flannel as last year,
the same hat as last week,
beards slightly thicker,
melanin slightly lighter.

We order three beers at a time,
each with his turn
leaving the twenty-dollar bill
accepting no change
only exchanging handshakes and smiles
with the bartender
whom knew we would arrive.
Our table outside we commandeer,
our territory, our barrel, 'ours' only
as much as the tree in the park
I write beneath;
our home-base where smoke

and laughs and satisfied sips coalesce
with questions and answers
about our steps, foundations,
cracks sutured or ripped wider apart,
our round table of ideas,
anecdotes, poems.
We share and listen with glinted eyes
slightly glossier upon each toke
upon each refill of golden haze,
as the sun slithers,
as the angst of unnecessary
anxieties dissipate.

For no matter the days that have been,
here over cold beers watching
leaves fall from trees
baring skeletal soul for all to see,
we, are at peace.

Once the bellies slosh
and hearts are spilled
away we go whence we came,
to see our lovers,
to cook some dinner,
to dive into another week.

(For my friends/brothers, Kevin and Seth,
thank you for your friendship.)

THE GNASHED

With the nonchalant-ness
Of mermaids long discovered by pacifists
As the seal descends
Into the ripple's nucleus
Killer whale north as the earth burns
Great White my smoke tonight
As is another New Englander's plight
Unicorns uniting by voice in the dark
Dinosaur bellow between cackling flames
Coyotes the mountain inside your legs
Kestrel the leaves of yesterday's dead
As a dog smiles with bloody licks
Pant – sigh – let the paws dry
Duck's laugh never the aftermath
To splash of claws once patient in dirt
Moon winks knowing we are all wild
And the alive are alive
And the gnashed have contributed

TAKE CARE
OF THIS PLANET FIRST

All the possibilities within the sky.
Dreams of perhaps,
maybe more.
A new planet for us?
Why must we procure?
When here upon earth
we slash and destroy.
Sci-fi fantasies within modern destruction,
We do not deserve another planet
If we cannot preserve our own.

I AM AN OWL AFTERALL

I like to sit outside late at night
And write poetry.
Everything hums a different beat, as do I.
I imagine things I simply cannot in the day,
In the busyness or expectation.
Everyone is asleep everyone is awake,
Everyone is learning. Evolution…
I see it gleaming promise despite
Wrenching growth pains.
I feel peace,
And too the rain drops on my skin.
Carnelian pleasure,
Petrichor nirvana.

THE GOLDEN HOUR

Ah yes
The golden hour
Whence the sun is nearly done
River rippling effervescently
Diamond-millions trading places
As fish feast and herons hunt
Eagles circle above until dusk
Tawny grasses reach for me
Or turn away depending
Which way I lay thirsty eyes
Flutter of leftover leaves sing
For the let-go already blown
Sagebrush scents drift thru me
West to the peaks east to the hills
Slithering upon cold facets of
Brown tacit time stood still

AS IF IT NEVER MATTERED

Upon the flat top plateau of a mesa
I see myself dancing emotionally
Meditating not stoically
As I nearly whoosh by.

Red teared me simply sand scattered
In the wind-scape of time, perhaps.

I turn truck to cliff,
Set shift to neutral,
One bag I throw out the door then I

Roll
Dirt rock punch slide

The truck disappears into the gulch
Silently descending then exploding
As if it never mattered,
I spit out sand-grit blood
Swallow some,

Disappointed vultures appear out of an
Indolent hell squawking ugly words
As I walk away,

Cigarette, limp,
An eye to I.

SHAN'T STAY HERE LONG

A cabin in the woods
Beneath steadfast peaks
Above the fickle khaki flat
Wedged between the steep
On a lodgepole slope
Uphill downhill it has both

Mountain mule kicked in the wall
Porch avails to pinecone gravity
Tin pipe no longer connects
Grumpy stove to moody sky
Here snow creates a slide

It seems as if only ghosts
And occasional lion
Likens this cave
Now but a crumple
An age beyond forgotten duff

A gold miner's boot
Somewhere in rot

LET IT BE & THEN REMEMBER

There will be days
when the sun of your heart never shines,
when rain no longer cleanses
only saturates and weighs.

There will be invisible blankets not
allowing soul to breathe,
choking out purpose
suffocating vigor
drowning life
and yet,
those days shall not last.

For today I say, "I reclaim me!"

I remember who I am and what I must do,
I remember why I am I,
I remember my worth,
I return to the fight.

MIDNIGHT WORDS

It is late, yet, I cannot sleep,
the owl in me has much to say,
all of day seemed to wait
to run this mind beneath the moon.

Frost has set upon pine needles,
lover lays blanketed, cocooned,
but I can't even close these eyes
for when I try, life reignites.

I know that if I relax each muscle,
think of all I'm thankful for,
then in time sleep shall come
as a boy whose mother hums.

Lo this known nocturnal dance!
I the fox in a mole-ish trance,
needing to bleed out midnight words
in order to rest and rise again.

9:39 PM

The moon shall be full at 9:39
here where I stand upside down
or slanted
somehow -upon this globe.

At 9:38 I shall look up into the wrap
of light swaddling tonight
silhouetting trees now with no leaves
battling the mist
whence winter winds wispily wiggle in,
as the climax intensifies.

The Beaver Moon
of Thanksgiving Thursday

The Frost Moon
of hibernations tone

The Mourning Moon
of shadows long pon empty streets
wearing the shuffle of
autumnal dissipation.

The moon shall be full at 9:39
to bathe the gratuitous beat
of preparation,

shriveled cacti,
illuminated eye.

ELIMINATE

To vociferate this soul thru eye
Not in tears welled – scraped from wall
Or gasps refilling eternal spills,
But in quivering awe
Of pure humble life.

Enigmatic grays pierced by light
Striking earth with tender might,
Crumpled trees reach as
Animals walk, chins lift
To mother's talk.

Soul-chaff finally caught in wind
Litter shaken from yesterday
Dissipates to corner's
Forgotten common
Decaying stench,

I the disease I eliminate.

TIL WELL PAST NOON

Take my hand
and hold it tight

We've a valley
to explore this night,

Over there
beyond the sun

Whence our dreams
have begun.

Wrap your leg
don't let it slip

While winds do try
to pry our grip,

For in our warm
cotton cocoon

We could sleep
'til well past noon.

HOUSE HOLDING SHOULDERS STRONG

This house makes its own sound
Boards built in certain ways
Rain drips there now
It didn't before
When only trees were here
When the boards were trees

Wind battles to get around
This house holding shoulders strong
Groaning like morbid lovers
Harkening heckles from zephyrs
Like teenagers with mailboxes
Smashed scraped never-ends
Slithering into adulthood sneakily
Suddenly hurricanes or tornadoes
Ushering in greedy liars

Maybe this house didn't want to be here
In the first place

Maybe the winds have reason to be angry
I believe they do

But for now
I am thankful – house –

That you are here
Whine on creaky castle
Wine on

CROSSWORD AT THE BAR

It aint a busy night
which we like,
two seats wooden bar
next to leg-lamp light.

A Christmas Story
another December
laced n webbed or maybe purled,
we ponder all the words
we can remember.

Whiskey hot n whiskey ice
beers to tend internal sweater,
sybaritic sauce
sustenance treasure,
balance of everything
isn't it?

Libras in lock
lips on lips reposit.
We've an eye for eye
we've the pen to our soul,
so, let's fill these boxes
as fire emboldens.

BREATH OF BREAD

Here in the bakery
early December

Where only t-shirts and flour
need to be worn

Early afternoon sideways sun
loaf after loaf pulled from hot oven
cooled upon racks
yeast scent warm in the air
breath of bread medicating
outdoor chill

Each time the glass door opens
bells jingle, another patron
seeks asylum,
crisp icy sabers pierce
the pillar of 'in here'

But only for a second, as the
warmth of bread's birth
overpowers any shiver

SNOWY SLUMBER AFTER SLEEP

I awake from a deep evening sleep,
the kind only a docile daze
after Christmas can lend,
to see the earth is covered
with just a little bit of fresh snow.

In an entire new globe, I now live,
as an old man awoken in new rebirth,
as a beard blossoms
in Rip Van Winkle dreams.

Within my sight no footsteps are seen,
only the mirror of moonscape
untrodden wilderness
of timeless blink.

The sky has mellowed to one last
snowflake flutter, easing upon the crust
sliding tenderly down tendrils
as I had fallen into that sleep.

My breath rises past the flake
up whence it came, t'ward the veiled
gentle glow of heaven's milky eye.

CHACO AND I

Chaco seemed to give no fucks,
but I could tell that he was sad.
A rascal horse dark muddy brown,
no manicured champ like his dad.

Here on this ranch each new steed,
more fit, taller, striking than yore,
so, who has time for stubborn Chaco,
let him roam out on the moor.

Flowing manes, bedazzled dames
money scattered like alfalfa,
fancy saddles, bridled bays,
I must go see the forgotten alpha.

Through the lea, earth painted jeans
with carrots, calm and empathy
I found Chaco, tail swishing irked
chocolate wile in summer's green.

Upon my entry to his realm he
turned and galloped to the trees
looking astern all that way
to see me lounge, laugh at his craze.

"I'll wait for you to come back!
aint chasing you 'round again,

but if you want, I've got a snack,
then you and I let's race the wind!"
Before smoke ascends to heaven
Chaco astutely slinks cross the lea
his muzzle sniffs my earthen lean
lips smack my hat friend-lily.

We eat a carrot each, dusty duo,
tacitly understanding pain
considering social adjustments
emboldening grit 'pon internal stains.

There is no time for wallowing
let's race the winds bareback free
forget the soul hurt wrenching,
disappear as lore, a summer's dream.

INSANELY ME

Barely rain, nearly snow,

night is melting, candle wax drip.

If this brain could please slow down

I wont slip deeper into the drown,

and yet

I am free here,

in a place unattained by peace,

in a watercolor drenched.

Tendrils of sanity emancipated,

I am me.

LISTEN TO EACH NOTE

As a boy they would sit me down
my face to window or wall,
it did not matter for vision
was to be meditation of sound.

Classical music was then played,
Beethoven, Tchaikovsky, Bach,
grand concertos with all the tools
to paint any audible fantasy.

It was up to me to dissect
each instrument's singularity
supporting the rest, all for one
orchestra coalescence.

And then to the piano I'd turn
to recreate each building stone heard,
just beginning to learn what
character and community meant.

A NEW WAY

Ol' gray truck, all banged up,
Dropped down Oregon crevasse,
Fist fights o'er whiskey and worse,
Star-dizzied under stars,
Bears silent, tho toes touched
The berries they would eat
Next morning before summer heat
Rose and blazed upon our faults.

Truck is dead, swallowed
By forest. Sugar Pines, Madrones,
Myrtles and Firs all rooting grip
Around gray rhino once was;
A new road must be built to drag it out,
A new way of life must be sought now,
As the canyon is the river is the rain,
It is time, to mature from this pain.

FORGOTTEN LEAVES

Frozen trees still
The mist
An agent of gloom
Mystically enticing
Confusing convincing
Souls to shutter shut
And mimes to wink
As foxes circle in dens no more
Tacitly dead
To me
To her
To the shuffle disrupting
The secret
Knife in a dream
Mimicking broken glass
Scattered in moon's gleam

It is silent tonight
Breath of meditation success
Death an eternity
Of forgotten leaves

GRAZES, RETRACTS

Shifting softly to the side

Hip slipped asleep
Lover's love dripped astray

Latch of sylvan gate
Ruling spirits in a pen

Rustily grazes then retracts

Unbinding all boundaries
Of what one once believed

In the wind billowing
In the tree's pinecone release

Earthen metamorphosis

History deceased

WARM WINTER DAY INTO NIGHT

A January day
surrendering freeze
in this valley
below the mountains,
large tawny swath
speckled dark green
warm beneath
snow laden peaks,
river of mirror
snaking between.

Yet as the sun sets
leaving east blue and west
a dimming orange crest,
the valley
tightens its muscles,
mud hardens as stone
and puddles glisten like eyelids
slipping to rest.

NIRVANIC PLACE

Walking downhill
thru thinning pines,
a pause to peer
upon meadow ahead,
into tall lush grass
verdant scratch
hugging my legs.

I bathe slowly
waiting
holily placed,
a sacred ant crawling
across a nirvanic place.

Oh, wind whistling thru the grama
you bend the faces of trees
leaning
withers of once wavering
in deer shadows
in badger holes
in stars shining on certain nights

whence moon has disappeared
behind the hills,
whence the wind
becomes still.

KEEP CARRYING YOURSELF

I carry myself everywhere I go,
for I contain all I need.

I contain all I am.

Along the way I see you,
you inspire me,
living everyday life
doing what you must
carrying all that you need.

When I meet you
in a tavern or a meadow
we may seem rough around the edges,
for that is how we are.

Yet when we meet,
we take a moment
looking upon the other,
humming ethereally,

you being you, and I, me.

FERAL JUICE

Rudder-ed by zealous passions

Preserved by also reason

Vined within a jungle of

Mind's ubiquitous season,

Soul forever tormented

In millstone barley grind,

My art the feral juice

Of an earnest Mortimer mind.

ROAN HIGHLAND'S CROON

Upon misty Roan Highlands
Where tawny blades blend to blue,
I saw the man with long gray beard
In brewing storm of afternoon.

He had a pipe which didn't smoke
Hanging from hidden left side lip
Between long hairs that had grown
Smirking between earthen tones.

Before I approached any closer
I halted, listened to all sounds,
He whistled a song to dappled horses
Grazing wild on gust-whipped crown.

Whoosh and melody all combined
Whirlwind mountain above the trees
Lullaby fades indigenously,
Ol man who died but never leaves.

HERE I CAN BREATHE

East of town, away from river's carve and ponderosa palisades // beyond the streets full of cars seeping gasoline fumes // past the rooftops harboring televisions and microwaves // across gradient of juniper space wearing paw prints of coyotes, lions, hares // here in lush-dry dance of winter immersed in the melancholic resiliency of sagebrush // I can see the majestic moody sky in a grander way // ambient to my eyes, no boughs above to impede // the immortal outer space bowing down to blow upon my nose // shoulders square to south // from east to west cumulus and nimbus beasts billow // shifting, spurting snow sporadically across horizon // sunbeams slice through the planet's wizardly beard like heavenly sabers as the wind moves the world // as everything moves // as the sage beckons me to dive into the dimension of eternal truth // unspoken knowledge of wild soul.

LIONS AND GHOSTS

I often think about the mountain lion,
walking thru town down the alleys I do,
late at night like I, behind the deer
tenderly touching ice, unlike I,
indigenous winter tread, ballerina
to my plodding rubber sleds.

I think about the ghosts I sometimes see
in peripheral vision, quickly,
then gone into the dimension I focus on,
nocturnal pacers, perhaps, like the lion,
reposed at day like the lion,
alert from twilight 'til twilight.

I wander pondering all this at night
to rail against the angst breaching,
sirens seducing my earthen tread,
I will drown they know if I am not lured
enough so, by the midnight wonder
of all mysterious beings.

SAD SON

Don't lick my under-orange-peal,
its citrus is sweat of insolence
maturing as canyons do.

Tumbling rocks thrown by tourists
educated by collateral damage,
my mother wise and sad,

son on soil, ruddered by soul,
the one the matriarch
could not control.

I picture her hair turning to gray,
her face I've kissed once
in nearly a decade;

Oh, woman who birthed me,
wayward son to mother afar,
it is from you, I evolve.

MY HEART IS IN
THE DESERT TONIGHT

I think of the desert tonight
as I drink a cold beer
in colder air enveloped in white.

As I look up into cloud-tears
meandering down weary pines
to join the trillion others, and I,
I imagine the desert softening
into purples, fading into silhouettes
sharp against a pin-hole heaven.

Here the world is frozen
dressed as a hermit's mirage,
horizon and wind wrapping ponderosas.
But in the desert snow amplifies
a salient earth, as frosting upon
a southern red velvet cake.

Winter here, winter there,
blanket swaddling my horripilated soul,
water gushing down into browns.

Upon my first trek across untilled breadth
I carried my heart north to here,
and now, my heart is in the desert.

A FATHER'S LOVE

It was long past his bedtime,
It was colder than zero,
His father's footsteps creaked
On kitchen floor beneath.

Out his window earth glimmered
Full moon valiantly soaring,
Midnight venture commence,
To spot the snowy owl.

Bundled in adrenaline
Layers of cloth as armor,
Father and son set out
Into the wild winter.

Crunch down dark street to the trail
Moonlight beams slipping thru trees
Into the deep gently,
Frigid winds whispering.

First words spoken by the boy
A mile into the wild,
"Father here we will sit
And see the snowy owl."

There beneath a hemlock tree
On edge of frozen meadow,

The son silently knew
That his father loved him.

I WILL NEVER BE LIKE YOU

You want me to tear the thorns
out of my side,
become a better rose,
be more fitting for your personal vase?!

You want me to be an ideal me,
as you see it,
neglecting all reasons, I am me?
Forget the savage,
forget the remains of older generations,
forfeit ideals forged by mountains
you millwork
naively tending with a civil touch
trying to wipe out the rough
sneering at the gruff,
attempting to bend my arm
in a way it doesn't bend,
as you filter water and tremble at bears,
as you litter your trash everywhere.
Hershey's I'll never know yee,
supplying candy that upholds child slavery.
Anaconda of the half face,
suffocating an honest place,
the filth I defy
may not be the 'filth' you wish I would,
as I strive to better the whole world.
I am a warrior of wilderness

beyond what you imagine.
I will never be like you.

THE TRANSITION

Today sun shone brightly
Bluebird skies and only
Fingernail moon

Sun set into dark clouds
Slithering oozy way
Over mountains

Wind's emboldened vigor
Whooshes into village
Triumphantly

Screen doors on porches creak
Dogs sleep one eye open
Supper simmers

A snowflake and raindrop
Argue their way to earth
Truculent love

Fingernail moon no more
Just the gray bluster of
A tempest's skirt

PUMA PROWL

Tussle my tenacity // if it comes to that
Though I hope not // those claws and teeth
That muscular body

It has been 5 hours // since we've never met
As you follow me // my soul horripilated
My senses afire

In my tread // in my tracks
Above my head // lurking rocky ridge
You are hunting me

Muzzle moist // claws ready to retract
Yet I keep turning // and singing to you
Wherever you are

You peer down on me // upon my passion
Upon my curiosity // coy like the cat you are
Patient enigma of verity

YES I AM

Some days, ya gotta say "fuck it"
and take the dollars into
a fancy place, sit at the bar,
drink a beer and whiskey,
look around, be looked at,
examine the menu, write poetry
in a ratty notebook
out of a ratty pocket.

I stink, probably, I hope so.

Some cat in here with
gray short hair named Harold
recognized me. "Wing!"
He hollers full of wine
and finest rib-eye.
"Wing, you are the poet!"

"Yes," I say,
a long sip of whiskey,
"yes I am."

DIRTY DAYS ON THE FARM

Everybody put twenty on it
that I couldn't pick up that burro,
outcast guy for a heave-ho
me in a similar boat.
Stubborn ass I fed each day
always trying to kick when
I'd feed, or halt when I'd lead,
I'll pick that mongrel off his feet.

A jolly eleven gathered around
as I tightened my overalls and
sloshed through slop to the gray
Eeyore obstinate, hoofs in mud
eyeballs like a moon in pollution.
He knew me well, too morosely
mildly humored to move, so
I sidled close, body harnessing.

Everyone cheered at this move,
I the muddy sporting fool, arms
wrapping coarse belly breast of
a hairy ornery nihilist beast. He
bellowed, I did too, we snorted
in tune, then in wild-west destress,
sunk into intrepid boots, I
heaved that bray to the moon.

THE MIRAGE IS YE

Silhouettes upon sand dunes
Kokopelli dancers in slow motion
Whittling dimension
Sun flower seed-spitters or
Ghosts playing with spiders
Blue Whale breach
Eyeball pierces soul
A mile out into
Horizon's chance
Sinking with the sun

Oh, treeless place, wavering
Landscape in between
The dunes and eternity
Cosmic underbellies
Wearing tentacles
The tenacious fight
To survive beyond
The not quite end

Never seal the shutters
Eye of shapeshifter
The mirage is ye

MAYBE BLUE

Sit up kid,
You last spoke too long ago,

It's time to tell them
What emotion you are feeling,
According to that chart of clowns.

Where you going kid?
I'm talking to you!
~
Spun in speedy existence,
Somewhat sweet a cover up

Out of breath, deflated waystation,
Forgetting to ask all's forgiveness

Maybe blue, if azure is sinew
A tornado of life lives twirled

Eternally eruditional crescive me,
In this vehement swirl
~
So many poems
Like birds that fly by.
Never to be seen again?

Dash of brilliance

Lost in existence?
Peripheral Equivocal Syntax.

ANIMA SURGE

Late night beckons me
with a dark whisper,
a slithering under-lord
to daylight's fetter.

Hench of persuasion
like a siren song,
umbilical equation
born before dawn.

A cape of freedom
she seems to display,
sapid shadows tug my soul
luring word play.

Gentle tongue twirl
creating an urge,
'til the primal explosion
of anima surge.

WE ARE NOT BOUND

They settled down the river softer
then the river raging,
into lands sacred,
taking advantage of, again,
oblivious,
as if
"God said so."
Fools, I say,
it was white supremist greed I say,
yet here I am,
born a strange mule of dimensions;
always fluttering to be
-true

Dripping
Water
We
Erode
Verity

Yet we do not have to.
We are not bound to history's sin.

A REMINDER

Watching a lightning storm to the south
All night
Like a vampire sucking maroon and silver
Vibrations
Sinking into my soul then seeping out
The rumble
Crawling thru trees and shaking my face
Reminding
Of horror on this earth we must eliminate

DISMAL

The half pint of beer in my hand was still cool // tho I had not raised its lips to mine in some time // too focused upon the lone goose in field // standing on one leg // looking far into the horizon// as a dog may search for their master's ghost to possibly approach.

The sunset was caught by a net of clouds // The air once deceivingly yellow had turned to blue again // The only bird flying // a Swainson's Hawk heading home // leered down upon the goose stymied on one leg // and I // dismally holding my beverage.

ANOTHER POEM TO THE MOON

Seduce me moon
As you buff into your bloom
Slipping cross the sky
Zealous siren in mine eye

Slice the berry stars
On pilgrimage afar
Shivering souls deep
Of poets who cannot sleep

PACIFIC CREST TRAIL MORNING

Dawn is and was. Cold unsliced
bagels for breakfast, salami,
cheese, figs, almonds,
whole powdered milk mixed with
spring water, instant coffee,
oatmeal, fair trade cocoa - wash it all
down. Set camp here the night
before cuz the moon was filling,
drank a bottle of whiskey,
to ensure I wouldn't fall off the precipice.

Danced like confident aspen leaves
hooting with owls and flying with squirrels
until my legs were as empty as the bottle.

The ridge I awoke upon and now
tread upwards, leads to a wide
rolling upland of satiated
grass and flowers. I will eat
lunch there, and maybe nap or
write poetry. If the clouds
billow much I will stay for the
night, tucked in the folds of
floral rainbows; if the sky
provides promising peace,

then perhaps tonight
I shall summit the peak.

BETWEEN SLEEP AND AWAKE

It is not time to wake
and if I have, I'm not yet sure
tho I know the warmth of
your skin all along mine,
as if melted together in the night.
We've each breached frill with foot out free
beyond tangle of blankets our legs become,
our hips swiveled as flower petals embrace,
our arms and necks entwined
between pillows parted by bed teased hair.
It is not a dream I now know,
for the lea we were in was far too cold,
colder than the swaddle of all-night skin,
your lips slightly apart
hallowing peace upon my nose,
your eyelashes my eyebrows,
your toes my achilles,
my heart within your clenched fingers.
I open my eyes just barely enough,
to see your carnelian glow;
dark blue hews passively tap
on the nebulous window curtains beyond;
our distance is none,
our temple is one,
and in a puissant wave
of grateful love
flourishing throughout my all,

the weight of sleep
drags these eyelids shut again.

STRIKE ME AGAIN

They must not know who I am,
He thought, as they yelled at him,
Spewing admonishing bullets which
Could not penetrate, only scathe,
Their own respect he once held
Now disintegrating rapidly.

They must not know this is not
How I learn, nor how one should teach,
The hand of anger striking again
To which callouses form, strength
Not severity, patient kind regard,
The teacher a student, now dead.

BELLOW

The roar of the ocean altered everything,
monumental at first,

like hot water jumping in
'til running thru trees
and sliding down scree
hanging from a bough as a monkey might,
staring into the end and beginning,
bellow captivating all senses and morphing
my once-was into a new truth.

I made it to the tawny sanctuary
of sand-dunes
always shifting into a new state of peace,
the ocean's roar now a part
of me once more,
my soul now salty
with sentiment and heroism.

My body but a flake of end and beginning.

My passion a light house
thru darkest storm.

THE LAST CANDLE

of tonight is not yet extinguished
for we've still water glasses to fill
and blankets to turn down, and us
to crawl into bed.

The candle upon piano flickers,
casting figures foraying wall
with rascal silhouettes,
fiery infatuates daffily imparting
the jettison of conviviality;
day dreams evaporating and
dancing with nocturnal delicacy.

I lean beside you, your head upon
the hand I will use to write this note,
your breath ahead of mine
nearly grasping essence of deep repose.

I hardly move, to not disturb
the simmered brio we are swaddled in,
this grandest of all joy's feelings
the peace of being next to you
beneath this day's last candle
lovers consecrated in love.

SO QUIET

It is so quiet
I can hear a washing machine
down the street behind a wall,
footsteps shuffling further beyond,
the growl of my lover's
snores through the cottage door,
the trickle of a broken leaf still
limping since last autumn,
the rearrangement of a nutshell in a nest
the wisp of a curtain breeze
the sigh of northwest sweet corn,
I can hear food ghosts
escaping a curled coyote,
between a racoon's intentional steps
and the waspy hum of electricity,
between my finger on this note
and a big wheel trucker maybe never
heading home, apparitions
of each age sliding each
their own way, audibly aware,
in a silence so quiet
I hear everything.

MANTA RAY

An old hippie RV is on the move,
chugging its way around the
neighborhood, at this 'all's well' hour
of sleep disturbed, like a manta ray
begrudgingly relocating;
perhaps a shark slowly drove by,
scanning its bored harassing light,
looking for trouble, looking to ensnare.

Then move on 'ol Manta Ray RV,
I don't blame you, if the sharks won't
stop circling these dark cranny streets,
there is a wide-open sandy wash ahead,
a parking lot in which you can blend,
where no sharks shall feast
upon your peace tonight.

AT GRANDMA'S HOUSE

A tortured soul roaring
before a wide-open field
veiled in fog not yet dawn

theatre of fuliginous monsters

bottle of wine half shattered in hand
tears streaming down cheeks
coalescing with sweat
with cigarette ash with the soil
covered in pecans
beneath the only tree around.

In haze of state lines
all the beasts howl
vying for my soul.

Sirens suck the mortar
'tween my bones,
'til these molecules I am
are rearranged.

~

I awake before noon sizzling in hot sun,
the shade of the tree, behind me.
The only cloud now, myself,

exhausted, confused, still alive.

The ants crawling all over my body
draw my first smile, and the dogs
still there by side, bewildered by
what I had become in the fog.

I let the ants and the sun and
the licks of the pups forage all
of my negativity, washing away
the soot of transmutation.

I must go see grandmother now,
fix the fence, clean the workshop,
tell her truthfully, I will be alright,
and then eat banana pudding.

My heart bleeds too much,
my soul senses too strongly,
a voodoo doll to the world
tied by ethereal threads
I burn and writhe within.

Why why why do I pour
any essence into the
millstone of nightmares?

I must meditate more,
lean harder into myself,

to calm this incineration
within, to numb the
displeasure of me,
as wet concrete
poured and patted
to be silently trodden upon.

OM

It doesn't need to be fancy,
just a walk in the woods,
a chance to talk together
about who we are
and how best to grow.

Lines between commenting
upon devolving light on trees
a sailor quietly whistling a lullaby,
or the vastness above,
we but pioneers
cloaked as laughing birds.

It doesn't need to be fancy,
nothing ever with you
needs anything,

for simply your essence from
honest simple existence

is a treasure
which illuminates my soul
filling my peace with Om.

BIRD PARENTS

The rain has come as a deluge today.
Periodical bursts of roof patter,
hood drench,
post-run-cleanse not yet home
shifting across the land
as a knight on a chess board,
great spillage of gray-blue arm
fallen off bed-edge,
fingers shifting asleep holding onto nothing
everything let go.

The birds take breaks from resourcing
during the downpour,
a family having nested in roof.

Everyone is home when the sky fall groans
bold chirping babes with impatient craves.

The dog tilts her head
as curious dogs do
looking up to yellow corner of living room,
she seems to understand
we have squatters on hand,
but better than the wasps
who first considered same spot.

The parents have flown

back into the rain now a dissipating drizzle,
the roof not a drum once again.

BABEL TOWER

There is that growl of thunder, grumble of
god-ish constipation loosening, maniacal
grind of rabid beastly jaws, frothing at
lips, dripping ever closer, advancing with a
Komodo Dragon red eye evil swagger.

I knew it would come, beyond the
bluebells of morning's sunlight love,
beyond steam rising like ethereal bodies
of yoga flowers, unfurled swanly posture
from drench of valley's yesterday.

Peering upon western horizon, with coffee
beneath tree not yet trembling, I could see
great castles begin to billow above the
mountains, giants having crawled
around the world to enter this one again.

Empires of intention reached Babel Tower
heights 'til holiness could no longer be
considered holy, spilling into grays,
lashing across the valley, claws slashing
terra, soon to drag across my face.

SIMPLY TRUE

At the end of each day,
after all summits and storms have
adorned their crowns,
after valley's warm sun wakening has
danced until trees bow to the night,
whence all has been
for the day that was,
only now, in the consideration,
nay the ceremony of completion,
do colors such as these
bleed out of soul.

A purge so heavy
it can be neither right nor wrong,
simply the culmination
of 60 tornados a minute
for all hours on end,
until now
bathing in ebony grains of existence,
releasing the song I must release,
always sui generis,
never right nor wrong,
simply true.

EXPONENTIATE

I can feel the spirit of outrageous souls,
pioneers in air,
in this growing summer heat
Tubman's and Cassidy's whirl about,
as they once did, as they always do,
for a soul does not die,
it is simply freed to be
as molecularly magical
as it wishes itself to be,
taking on cyclones and sea-crossing winds,
embedding themselves in babes
ideas
craves
in horrendous impassions like me.

There is no torch to be passed
for it only multiplies
exponentiates,
a true eternal flame
wilder each epoch.

DRIPPING MUSTARD B.C. (BEFORE COVID)

It is the perfect kind of Saturday
where cars are parked
deep into neighborhoods,
lining the streets where homeowners
will place their trash bins on Monday.

Hoards of hand-holding
Cargo-short couples,
kids smacking shoes on sidewalks,
compadres already swaying
from extended brunches,
masses of uniques and alikes
all descend upon downtown.

Main Streets are blocked
off from vehicles,
now wearing cord-snaking-stages
wearing instruments and amplifiers
and revolving musicians,
food carts and artist tents line
the fracas of cattle-like-humans
milling vacationally
everyone meandering as if
they have forgotten time
and commonsense,

spinning wheels, dripping mustard,
screaming above cover bands,
stopping suddenly,
throwing trash at bins they miss,
for the town pays someone to pick it up.
It is the best kind of Saturday,
for as we walk through all the mayhem,
we finally reach the edge, and home.
We take off our day clothes,
let our skin breathe,
open windows for breeze,
kiss between puffs of marijuana
and vhino verde sips,
we cook dinner in peace,
lovers in laughter,
away from the pandemonium
of summer USA.

DON'T

Why did you kill the people already here?
Why is Indians and Cowboys
a classic childhood game?
Why is murder the smirking corner
of our greatness?
(In folklore, in speak-soak, in child-food)
Why is joining the Anarchists,
and fighting against equality
considered an honorable thing?
To be a pawn for the elite,
to carry the guns of evil souls
saluting a flag
like good citizens as told,
to make money for demons –
why do you obey the oppressors?
Why do they,
the wealthy, humans financially capable
to heal this world, leave them all hungry,
naked and cold?
Why do you listen to the bullhorns?
Why buy their non-fair-trade
greedy muddled bullshit?
Don't.
It is time to revolt.
Be a rebel.
Fuck off to the ways it is or has been.
Inequality is draconian.

THE POWER OF YOU

When I look at you,
it feels as if every star
is falling into my heart.

When you smile at me
and seek my soul with your eyes

each star inside me bursts into meteors
shooting back to the heavens.

I burn in and out
descending and ascending

stirring and exploding
for you.

CHARLESTON TO SAVANNAH

This isn't a good place to sleep
tho it has been days,
train shimmies
ice cubes melt quickly in glasses
forehead condensation
dripping into t-shirt shoulders
whooshing thru gnarled ghostly
mossy silhouettes.

The guys behind me
snort key-bumps of cocaine
trying to get me to partake
jabbing my neck
with questionable wild eyes,
my head already on fire
bewilderment enough,
my ass the crater-mirror
of pebbled ground afternoon
waiting for the train considering all life.

Now on the train
rumbling to Savannah
with a sticky stinky brain.

A cigarette out a window would be nice.

FATHERLY BEAM

My dog is lounging on the patio
On the chair I recently left

I watch her thru my bedroom window,
Her black body keeping my warmth warm

She almost knows I am here
Above, inside, peering down fatuously

Her eyelids rise once every ten seconds,
Searching for me while she sleeps

Breeze that glitters her ebony fur reaches
My nose beyond trembling curtains

A rush of love suddenly seizes my heart
That this selfless friend is my family

I stare at her so proudly with
Fatherly Beam until she's had enough

And prances and jingles inside
To find me

TEQUILA IN A CUP

It is drizzling summer rain
tapping upon elephant tapestry
as I tap away poetry and a letter
to an old friend.

Barefoot, with tequila in a cup,
warm sentimental heart
replacing melancholy.

Occasional passerby's slide thru
the alleyway just a fence away,
the dog looks up quickly,
I turn too, we watch the shape sidle
along thru each fence board slit,
vision sputtered
like the bike spoke's tick.

Once they pass, dog lowers head slowly
then sighs as she rests muzzle again
upon same lounge as I.

Her tiger eyes agree with mine,
there was no need to bark or shout,
this afternoon
there is nothing to worry about.

LOVERS IN GREEN

Chase me down

let our hats fly off
and fall where they will.

Take me by the shoulders,
the ankle, the waist,
tackle me
into the heather of earth's curves,
pin me in the secret,
ravage me in the feathers,
mimic the wind with me
to the rhythm
of our lost clothes at sea,
siphoning sunlight
morphing carnelian bodies
lovers tangled
swaddled in green.

UPSIDE DOWN

The train tracks sing
for you and I
Midnight Travelers
of the sky

The leopard shrill
of desert stars
Nocturnal Artists
Noir Bizarres

Lost in the field
with the towns
Face of Unknowns
upside down

FOR NOW

a strange dream
bed sweat

glass of water naked in the kitchen

demons haven't transitioned yet

bare body on cold cement
leave all lights off
fire the stubbed out joint

unforever isn't a word
suck the torch of pacification

relax
remember

for now

do not focus
upon Herculean tasks
simply exist and respire
write a poem
then go back to bed

WHY I AM ALIVE

If I was to die young,
I'd first need to play piano
in front of you, all of you.

If I was to die young
I would first need to pour my soul
out truthfully.

Misunderstood, madcap wild

brewing zeal
to reckon peace,
with tears attached
to each note,

laughter lacing every chord,
walls of angst
falling into forgiveness,

upon each stage,
in each tavern
in your living room
challenging us
smashing keys
destroying the furniture of ideals,
for us.

This I need,
for if I am to die,
I must first show you
why I am alive.

LAZE OF THE LAND

Dog days of summer
hang heavy into the afternoon
as the dogs lay heavy
in the holes they've dug,
as boots finally lay aside
soggy socks strewn nearby
as ice cubes in my glass
fade before I'm done,
like glaciers and polar bears
stumbling south to die,
puddles ascending
back to the sky;
voices subdued
return without care,
and naps only wear sweat-beads
or straw hats,
oscillating fan
or finally breeze
break the drench
of atmosphere hang,
rumble of thunder
far away bangs,
mirage's dimension
guns down day's tension.

Sirius has summoned
the laze of the land,

nudging all beasts towards water
conforming each midday surrender.
Only the crops now stretch
and the snakes have vigor
like the one psycho jogging in the sun
or the cow who haphazardly
sat on a bee,
but the rest of us,
we wait, we wade,
we embrace a siesta,
until the sun descends
and clouds gleam afire.

THESE SUFFOCATING WEBS

This poet has not been feeling like a poet of late, but more as a horizon after the fog rolls in, indiscernible, blotted out, perhaps not even there.

I have lost my vigor and I don't know why; I cannot even cry anymore after that night the dam broke within me and I wailed and trembled until the earth's core was no longer molten.

The well has not been refilled, it has lagged empty, stagnant, cracks growing larger each day, the planet – my soul, creating mine own grave.

For weeks my window curtains have not let sun in, I can barely speak when I try, when I sit at the table of fellowship I once danced upon, I only feel I've died.

Depression, I tell myself, always fades, the wind will come and usher out the fog, it always does, the horizon is never eliminated, it only hides time to time, I think I know…

Yet, I will not wallow, I will attempt each day to emancipate my anima from these suffocating webs, stripped of armor I force myself out into the mocking brio, I will not succumb.

RIGHT ABOUT NOW

He waters his roses each evening
right about now,
maybe he thinks the same
of my sun-west strolls.

His denim-cap brim
bows down to the flowers,
my metronome stride like
a clock-hand tells hours.

He wears a goofy smile
almost lost in time's space,
perhaps why he nods
like he knows my pace.

A patch of pride
after rambling sighs,
each as the colors
humbled from life.

One beard brown
one beard gray,
two different beasts
finding peace, own way.

"TRIFLES"

It is not the earth's fault.
It is not the sun who seeks to decimate,
or the land whom is too violent.

Fire is not the evil, as it scorches
and devours trees we need,
oxygen we need. This is all our fault.

It is not simply 'the way things are'
that hatred must exist,
that bigotry and racism reign

that greed is simply the history of us.
Excuses against ourselves a catalyst,
transgressions we create and uphold.

As the world burns, we battle
beneath ominous skies obsessed
with trifles that do not matter.

The true "trifles" shall decide
each of our futures, the action of love,
selflessness, kindness, forgiveness,

the "trifle" of coming together in peace
to save a world responding as
white blood cells respond to disease,

all obstinance to this we must
immediately get the fuck over.
It is time to save the world from ourselves.

LIKE SEEDS

I am naked in the wheat field
I always drive by.

Tawny tears to purple dawn,
Spreading mud upon my face.

Take me further into the dark,
Try to kill me.

Suffer and live with the
Steadfast peace of forgiveness.

As we harvest our strength
Let us blow the truth
Of each other
Like dandelion seeds.

MORNING REVEILLE

The barn was not heated
and so,
at night the doors must always be shut
and the windows
between each stall and wind-whip
latched,
body heat of 27 horses
keeping each other alive.

I rolled up in the morning,
stalemate with twilight
beating the cock
waking the beasts
tire crumple over snow
fresh inches upon ice pack,
the barn a steaming glow
of hungry kicking nostrils.

The thermometer outside glinted -9;
I tried to slip my cold key
into the frozen lock
but it stymied.

I bent down close to the portal,
breathed fervor into its puzzled tight slit
until warmth and drip emanated.

I sucked out the melt
and slid the key gently in
turning it successfully,
opening the creaky icy door,
slipping my body into the dark musky barn.

27 dragons now awake
Whinnying
Wild
Zealously stomping
Sassy
Starving
Magnificently snorting.

FOXY

A cunning thing
the fox is,

Stealing my heart
and then

Giving it back to me.

THE HAD-ENOUGHS

When I look at the stars tonight
I imagine the great storm
churning across the islands,
heading toward the mainland
where wealthy leaders imbibe and laugh
whilst trading children for carnal sins,
and the poor working masses
humbly tremble
clutching their babes and pets.

I think of sinking Jakarta,
with 9 million more scrambling to relocate
never to push back time,
never to undo what has been done,
never to escape a fate we have all
prescribed with our actions.

I think of the rhino alone beneath
a Serengeti sky, I wonder if he cries.

I can smell the Palo Santo as it disappears
into the universe, earthen lungs
gasping, desiring to survive.

I can see the polar bear almost giving up,
its bones no longer held together
its soul seeking peace from pain.

I can hear the gunshots
and another mother's shriek

and the wailing mind
of nightmares inside cages
cold and crowded and confused
torn away from love for no fault.

A cancerous moon of victorious demons
wraps the world with blasphemous hymns
hoisting the religion of hateful destruction,
playing with the globe as evil puppeteers
they assume to consume all morality.

Yet they will succeed no longer.

For, as I look at the stars tonight,
I also hear the howls of The Had-Enoughs
the ripened fruit of zealous souls
rising to decimate all hate.

The world shall repair
what we have done here
and there are many of us
that fight with Her,
so that all may fall asleep feeling nourished,
safe,
with family,
at peace,

each human and organism
all of our very own home Mother Earth.

ARCANE LAYERS

The bear before me did not flinch
as a train far below in the valley
blared out a beckon which somehow
slithered its way up the mountain to us.

The bear just stared then paced between firs
before darting forward aggressively
as a coyote dares to play
yet doesn't quite trust.

Each of our chins
dripped from same waterfall,
each of our gruffs born
from sun-moon struts;

souls connected as a siblings split at birth,
so, neither of us needed to kill the other.

And though I invited him
to smoke some ganja,
he declined,
slinking away as a bear does,
into arcane layers.

CUT THE RIBBON

Where have you gone?
Lifeline light in the cave,
no longer glimmering
in the distance, only darkness.

Are you forever gone?
Is it now up to me to
contend with the eternal,
with only, that life of lessons

in this darkness?

I bite upon the charcoal you once licked,
nights of education, always passionate.

I slide my way thru the tunnels you would
harshly lead me down, trusting in your
departure as a fawn's first night alone,

believing in something I cannot see yet
realizing, it was you who blinded me.

Torment of demons that feasted,

stabbing
slashing
munching upon my brain

licking
spitting
regurgitating me into me
until,
I burned you out,
fired by the atomic sparks
of a grinding millstone
destroying my once infested was,
yet your death unveils pandemonium,

or is it my death? And I the fire all along?

Perhaps the ribbon I have followed can be
cut and I will fall and all I thought, is not.

REMINDER

Sometimes

It all feels too fast,

And so

Ya gotta slow it down

And just be.

THOUGHTS OF FAMILY

I think of my grandfather tonight,
As the full moon fills the sky with
A blanket of translucent frost,
I wonder where he's travelled, dead for
Years yet here, intangible truth to me.

I think of my father, alive in the sky
Flying from one continent to another
Crossing oceans trusting machine
Peering down upon the beginnings
Of hurricanes, steadier than I.

My mother, tucked away in her verdant
World with hair tips that weren't even roots
Whence we last exchanged our brown
Eyes for the others, and held each other
Tight in a final embrace.

My grandmother, eternal soul of kindness,
Living stronger than memory's caliber,
The beat of family heart, undampable
Torch of home, the matriarch
Blessing each our craves to roam.

NOT AT THE CABIN YET

I sit peacefully in a corner
as autumn rolls in,
my back to a trembling tree,
a knife and fist on each side leering out
upon the first leaves to fall.
my dog paces back and forth
as my mind did earlier,
before I gave up
and let myself be.

~

I'm not at the cabin yet
the one of my dreams
with a typewriter upon
a wide porch in the rain
and nothing but trees
in all directions,

dash of my dog
running thru it all,
getting into a scuffle
with a bear, or coyote
requiring me to
charge into the blosh,
moccasins and axe,

but whatever the drip,
words will be plucked out
of all possibilities,

pandemonium thoughts
in the woods,
in the peaceful chaos,
twixted into a poem.

OH WHIRL-WIND WEAPON OF WISE

Pull me deeper into the forest

Show me what I do not know

Bind me with curiosity
Enslave me to mindful freedom

Nothing matters if I don't go

Stuck in woeful ways is
The fire I burnt yesterday

Smoke signals my ghostly ride
Above the shell I leave behind

AWAKE AT NIGHT

It takes some time
to wake up in the morning,
warming slowly thru the day
looking sideways to see straight,
the mind awaking at night.

For it is here,
as if trapped in a dark conscious
that light pierces this conscious
and all that has been
now finally can make sense.

Upon this mental freedom release,
I become all of the moments in the day
replayed in reflection;
dirty traveler picking up trash in the park,
his dog licking sore paws.
elder lady's words as I walk by
"in the means of moments, we are rich,"
purple hat upon her head, strong coffee
scent.

The evil in the hierarchy
mocking the zealous shouts
of pure young wise warriors,
billionaires greedily blowing
fuel into fire they created,

large displays of candy in season
sourced from slavery of children,
the cop staring at a booty
only to turn and slowly
follow her down the sidewalk.
My father's plane flying overhead,
oceans rising all around,
house-cats tawny and gray
lounging in places where
only we make eye contact.

All of this,
now at night
upon my walk or write or piano soul
expunge,
I feel in the deepest soul depths,
all of the facets of each complex day,
each bug within the walls,
each birdsong upon branch,
lover's rhythmic face wash splash,
giggles over one's own thoughts,
all moments, coalesce.

CLUB OF MANIAC PORCH PACING ARTISTS

Are you out there?

Do you bare your tongue to the hail?

Let it tear your taste buds?
Swallow your own blood?
And the rain! Family tear's falling
Down posthumous sky drains,

Wrapped in thrift-store-ware
Fingers weathered from piano note slams
Torn up from guitar strings and rocks
Throat scuffing up conversations with alien peddlers.

Are you tasting existence?

Is your anima naked?

Do you dare to let the wild winds dare you?

I'm not sure if you do
Sailor of sea not yet sailed
Wolf-child still living in controlled hell
Betrothed to a partner you must escape.

Violent regrets
The birth of all graves.

AUTUMN

In this autumnal crescendo
I shall transform into a blaze of color,
Like the maples,
Then shed all of my summer
And bare my soul to the world
Shamelessly again.

In the moonlight
I shall hauntingly glow,
An enigma only to the ones
Who do not look or listen.

TEAR ON A CHEEK

It is late and you are on the far side of the
bed, turned away from my too late words,
so I sit at the piano, staring at the keys after
the gentlest lullaby I could drip, a tear
down my cheek, wondering a wall away
from you, if you still listen.

The books and paintings piled up upon this
holy desk of us, reminds me of our
moments, of all great poems unwritten.

Cruising, laughing along the Oregon coast,
taking turns driving so each could howl out
the window and let salty air coalesce with
our teeth and happiness.

When we saw the old red barn set in the
fields amongst the stench of cow manure,
(which you know I've always appreciated)
sign nearly fallen off – ANTIQUES- we
peeled in spontaneously giggling, hands
clenched upon each other to never let go.
We met Nancy, we meandered the
arrangement of a thousand things and
purchased laminated place-mats, pencil art
of Arizona, your birth-land.

Adventuring together, we believed in no end, and I still don't, despite any wall between us, or any roll away sleep.

We have created so much as a team and I hope we are not done, yet whatever becomes, I shall always continue to drip lullabies for you, upon any piano I come across, as soft as a tear on a cheek.

THERE I MUST GO

In between the coyote yips are the stars,
veiled by the trimmings of godly beards,
as continents cover oceans and wars
speckle history, births and deaths.

Juniper berries occasionally drop, field
mice sprint, an owl turns its head the
other way around, I pull in as much air my
lungs can handle, tingle of damp meadow.

Tree silhouette encompass, friends of
different heights, each waiting to see what
I will decide, guardians of where I happen
to be, watching me when I walk away,

which I must – deep into the darkness we
pretend does not exist yet is the catalyst –
for all light. There I will go, and as the
coyotes sing, I shall howl along.

KILL WHAT KILLS

The ends of the earth
Have led me to here

Volcanic soul bleed

Herculean ideals the catalyst

Yore the ship I sailed
To this shore, upon which
I shall make peace,

If I try to kill me,
I shall kill what tries to kill me.

SEED

It's as if my eyeballs
Have a fishhook through each
Attached to a wall
Walking away from me

I follow as close as I can
To avoid the worst pain
Tripping constantly
Upon roots and bricks and wisdom

It is blind I must be
Suffocating desire
Turning memory into water
Into sustenance for growth

I shall not bleed out
When my eyeballs rip out,
For I am more than sentiment,
I am seed.

THE GATHERING

They visited me again,
all emotion gathered together,
myself alone – with all of myself,
waxing moon gliding thru night
as a tide dutifully crawls,

eyes closed, eye open, meditating,
listening, all essence letting,
suddenly – I felt they were here.
Slowly, I opened the oculars of
physical body, and greeted

the gathering that had arrived,
intangible aura of bodies, individuals
only in peripherals, lines of beings, souls,
bittersweet of flowers transitioned
transcending community dimensions.

I do not fear their tacit whispers,
they do not manipulate mine anima,
we sit beneath our star filled sky as a
peaceful tribe, as if we each
are the fissure of apparitions.

CONFINED

Too trapped
Too contained

Highways on both sides
Screaming at me all of time

I must break out
And get back to

Where I'm meant to be

I SUPPOSE

Breaking up is like October weather,
A transition that summons all seasons,
Golden memories showering down
Hail spitting upon my face
The sun the end of our embrace
Warm as the tears descending
Into earth – everything.

Breaking up in October is even worse,
Or maybe it is better, for when is
Ever the best time for anything?
The answer
Is always now – I suppose.

IT IS TIME

I haven't been able
to sit at home
for the walls are painted
with our memories.

I've run the routine
of drink and smoke
to a more extreme degree,
but that is not what I need.

At first, I'd say
I need you, but that isn't true,
for all this has reminded me
I am enough on my own.

Second, I may say
I need to cry on brother's shoulder,
and yes, at first, I must,
but it is now time

to face this home and my fears
and my inner pains
in a healthy manner.
It is time to mature.

PERTINENT

You know the story

It is of simply being you

In each of our own sputtered spoke ways

Cog of the wheel if you will

Or stave of the barrel

All of us

Pertinent

CONSPIRING

It has never been easy
For me to fall asleep at night

Ever since I was a young boy and
The creatures would shine their lights

In the corner of my room, demons
Always conspiring over a fire

The only time I've ever fallen asleep
With ease and peace and desire

Has been in the wilderness alone
Or laying down in bed beside my lover

And even then, in my repose-heaven,
I still some nights must battle demons

Loneliness borrowed

As if a book from the shelf

I put it back

And choose something else

DAY OF SADNESS

Some days
Are simply days of sadness
And that's alright

One can run
The angst out
At other times

Or immerse oneself amongst
Laughter in an attempt
To ignore the pain

Or one can even
Boldly deny
The balance of life

Yet sometimes you just need
To embrace all of the heavy
Feelings alone

Knowing that
If I did not feel this way
I could never feel joy again

STILL ALIVE

All trees have collapsed

I somehow have not died

Cave within destruction

Moaning gut of cauldron

Boiling over as lava spews

Warmth of comrade's prayers

Soaking into marrow

Tear stained king

Fighting for a new world

BEING SINGLE AINT TOO BAD

Laying in bed at 2:45 in the afternoon,
drinking a glass of Spanish red wine,
smoking an indica joint
watching the snow fall gently
outside my open window.

It is not quite winter but it feels as such,
now that it is darker
and the ground has frozen,
which means my favorite season
for creating art is here.

No constraints, no rules beyond moral.

I can pound on the piano
and howl out my soul
whenever I choose,
I can write poetry and prose
from 4pm to 6am,
I can lay in bed and contemplate everything
then jump up right before the tired sun
slips away somewhere beyond
the blanket of gray clouds
and burst into snow-covered streets
to run with my dog
until all of our hairs are frozen,
then make a long robust pot of stew

or chili
or everything else that is hearty
and thaws us out
to romp and write and howl all night.

SAVED BY A DRUNKEN FRIEND

My plan,
sing the damn karaoke song
light a joint after the second verse
and get kicked outa here again.

This fucking bar, the first one
where I now shouldn't be
for rabid writhing reasons,
yet I returned
for some friends asked me to.

I have no problem saying no,
I will nail your foot to the floor
if you push me too hard,
yet at times I must put aside
grievances for my friendships;

so, excited I became
demon returned
to the not-same heaven.
Ready I was, to sing my song
and get kicked out of this bar again.

Yet out of the window
upon the icy sidewalk

my friend has slumped.

He must be carried to a taxi
and then,
I should let go of this angst,
and just go home.

OUR ONLY TIME, A MEMORY

I've been standing here tryna hitch for a while, but once the sun hit and hours of no rides set in, I decided to walk across the street to the general store. Got a bottle of Jim Beam and slid myself beneath a tree.

Once the great star sunk and I was righteously drunk and stoned and opening a new packet of loose tobacco I exited the forest back to roadside, not a motor in sight, nor the sun, but I was just enough lit for possibility.

Now, time did not matter, only 5 trucks drove by over the hours, but I swigged and rolled cigarettes and believed, 'the universe sees me' and then suddenly in my dirty behavior, the lights of a possibility pumped brakes.

"Where you tryna go?" A big bold woman brassed. "I'm headin down to Redding" my grateful ass hoping. She chimed, "if you can tell me a story, get in the car, otherwise you haven't come that far..."

She had the knife of persuasion in her eyes so I climbed in her wagon ready for the ride. A grand story I told of traveling the mountains, talking with bears and diving into fountains of cold spring sirens and sage.

She never took her eyes from the road; she drove steady whilst chain smoking Marlboros. Occasionally if I was to ever pause to reach for some water or shed back a tear, she'd lean with her shoulder and chuck up the line,

"keep on talking kid, this is our only time."

RECYCLE TRUCK

It sounds as if a wildcat is screaming,
'tween engine thrust and brake,
every hundred feet,
shattering silence each 30 seconds,
yet even though
my dream hears a wildcat, I too
can feel the early day's dim light
pulling me back to reality.

Before I even open eyes
I know it must be the ish of 7am,
it must be a Tuesday,
and the wildcat is simply
the crash of all
the wino's empty bottles
falling into the recycle truck.

RAIN'S REMNANTS

The drizzle was only a subtle passing,
Like a deer's timid steps in the forest
And a silent silhouette of a lion trailing.

It came as a dream does, interrupted
By seeping light through curtains,
Cloud of smoke, vanishing illusion.

Its only trace is the glint of ground,
Sparkle of ebony tree limbs where
Moon can reach between leftover brume,

Petrichor essence amplifies oleoresins,
Thicker air as if in a breath and also,
The chair I sit upon to write this poem
Is wet.

TRUE BALANCE

Stare at the bleak naked tree
Stark against gray smothering sky,
Its raven lineament an entanglement,
Wiry branches shoot out in all directions
Like an artist who cares not what they think
Or the honesty of an intimate lover.

Staring at this winter beast, I see
What at first appears, imbalance,
Grand errant limbs protrude wildly
Carrying one-thousand tiny crooks each,
Rampage with a lean seemingly distorted,
Incongruous to all government;

This makes me stare more intently for
I begin to see its ardent soul within.
I realize there is no imbalance,
There is no pandemonium, it is simply
All the truth of its own time, this naked
Veracious tree unlike all others.

LIVING FOR WE

Waiting behind the curtain
to play piano next

As braces on teeth
construction of what's best

Rebellion
destruction of this government

Lighting fire to the curtains
behind the smoke

Forest too deep for you
where I drown

Torn up flesh
releasing breath

Living for trees

Living for we

GODDESS SOULS

Beneath tonight's dim moonlight
memories glide and whisper

Dulcet sighs, sorrowed laughs,
apparitions of the past.

There's a woman on each road,
one above and one below,

Birth until rebirth they hum,
goddess souls of my freedom.

PIANO GRASS

When I play piano
I am a child running thru tawny grass
Up to my waist
Surrounded by golden aspens
In all directions
I ripple with their quiver
With each blade bending breeze
I spin in all directions
Within an autumn sea.

When I play piano
I am transported into all time's dreams
Each blade of grass
Is another of me
Quivering golden directions
Of who I used to be,
Spun in the autumn
Born within all seas
I am the bending rippling aspen breeze.

NO MORE

I just can't do this anymore,
Heart yo-yoed
Slung into the swamp
Hollowed, shattered
Delusional fantasy
Eternal suffocation reality

Shivering alone in the cave

Nebula's enigmatic dissolve

Death of the world with a smirk.

DAILY HEARTBREAK ROUTINE

In our little cottage
tucked close to the gravel road
dog and I go about our days and nights,

with every car that rumbles by
we both lift our heads and listen,
then look to each other in gloom,

for each vehicle has its own growl
as we each have our own footsteps,
and with each drive-by, we listen for you.

When it could maybe be
we both jump up racing to the window
to peer out beyond the linen veil,

I lower my head to the dog, she whines
as I sigh, we both return to whatever it is
we are trying to distract ourselves with.

UNTO NEW LANDS

Though storms ravage in waves as
Explosions of life-colliding energies,
I can feel the wrath of this one
Beginning to pass.

The sails I scrambled to roll up
And tie down (lest I should
Be drowned within the tempest)
May now be unfurled again,

Hoisted to their intended position
To collect the wind of my soul
And chariot me
unto new lands.

ANATOMIZED

I suppose I've anatomized myself
In order to be here.

All my parts as one
Yearned for what life
Did not become.

Dissected
I shall grow

Slashed apart
I seek peace

In shambles
I will understand.

What is heartbreak?
When love still exists.

A HEALTHY LOVE

I need to feel loved
just as much as I need to give love.

It doesn't need to be from a partner
or a family member,
it doesn't even need to be
from a friend who listens and truly cares,
it doesn't need to be a friendly hello
and compliment at a market
or kind help from a stranger,
nor the camaraderie with a sad bum
on a sidewalk
basking in the November melancholy sun
silently sharing a smoke,

it doesn't even need to be from
the wellspring of love a dog overflows.

For though all that love is a beautiful gift

the love I need is much deeper,
as moon and stars
as God loves each of us.

It is love for myself
given to me from me I need,
an honest, kind, tough, challenging love

that expects and believes and forgives
to the utmost,
a healthy love that is not indulging
but true.
To be worthy of any other love
I must first love myself,
for as she said,
"I am my own and my own is me."

Is my heart even worth guarding?
When I fight for yours
giving you mine
only to be squeezed dry
then tossed aside?

It is.
I will protect and saturate myself,
within responsibility,
with life

as a warrior fights to live until death.

The pain reminds me,

I am here to guide,
be abandoned,
then trek with Christ by my side
eternally,
my heart full of love and peace.

WITH A LIMP

Into the highlands
With a limp
Old piano out of tune

Start a fire and dry out
Shiver steaming
Mountain lion observing

Standing up to howl
The echo
Cathedral hall rushing spring

Here I could die
Impossibly
Essence of life discovered

JEALOUSY

My dog sniffs me over
when I get home,
as if questioning me
as if I dated women
as crazy as me.

I picture Bukowski
lighting a cigarette
turning up Beethoven
and smiling as she screams
broken glass
we are twisted trees,
I'll play piano thru WWIII.

My dog knows
I've met other dogs,
she is outraged by me.

HAUNT OF MOODY NIGHT

Wind is curling trees
Into motion monsters breathe

Gargantuan silhouettes shiver
Beneath bold waxing moon

Great Archer of expanse
Wears speedy low cloud sashes

Molecular masquerade whispers
Secrets of the universe

HOW WE HANDLE TODAY

Though the fire ravages
We will bloom again
Emboldened

Though we cannot rewind adversity
We must use it as a catalyst
To grow stronger, more true

Recognizing atrocity
Fighting for change
Creating change intentionally
Evolving through words and action
As honest honorable stewards
Of our earth and ourselves

How we handle today
Will determine all to come

A DOG'S DIGS

The dog digs in the dirt intentionally,
To create a den
Or temporary bed
To warm up or down
To cool down or up
To bury a bone
Or find one she has already
Buried long before
Or release stress
And then transform
Into a sudden savage
To help me garden
Or excavate rocks
To create art
And even hide secrets

As she digs
I step back with a sense of pride
And admire her

She trots towards me
When she has completed her task

Tail up warrior princess prance

Her nose coated with earth

COMMON BOND

There is that spider
On the ceiling
Always watching me

I pause with my writing
To peer upon her
Gentle smile between tears

A common bond we share
We know we will not kill each other
Though we could

CARNALLY DIVINE

Let's go to bed
and eat chocolate together

The kind with a caramel filling
that sticks to our lips and chins
forcing us to giggle with
teeth and tongues
as we scrape and eat
and lick upon each other

Let's go to bed
with many logs on the fire
that we burn and sweat
and completely undress
and evolve as flames do
dancing entwined
carnally divine

Our souls the embers of life

MURDER ATTEMPT

Drugged
Abducted
Beaten unconscious
Taken by car out to train tracks
Dumped in the snow
Drugs planted in pocket
Water poured upon my torpid body in 13-degree air
Left to die bleeding
Unconscious
Freezing in the night

But I did not die
Somehow, I woke up
I could not move
But somehow, I did

Some have said I am strong
But that strength I know
Has come from God

CONCUSSED

Brain shaken as a snow globe

Unable to hold any vision

So, I write in fetal position

Writhing back and forth

With fists clenched to forehead

Pressing in upon pain that seeps out

TORMENT

Roll me forward like a cannonball
Blast me into obliteration

Pronounce your royal forces
As if the bass-line was assassinated

Curl me into your ear while we sleep
Dreaming combinations

Kicking buckets into glass walls
Orange faded Georgia tornado

Torment the yolk of passion
I and you, all of the universe

A REPRIEVE

My heart is always enlightened
when I come upon a meadow
in the midst of dense forest.

A reprieve from the tunnel
a reunion with the sky
an awestruck saunter through the world
standing slow feeling everything that is life,

unshrouded of fear for death
humbled by the power
of this tinseled blithesome meadow.

I AM HOME

The air is thicker at home
Perhaps the slaughter of hearts
Or the hunt of my death

Either way when I return
Beneath the jungle thickets
Which do not guard

My gun my ax my tenacity to live
Stir the sauce and let it breathe
Sink into my tenacity

I am home.

Come try to kill me again
While I whisper upon the piano

I shall stab your brain

For I am home.

PURPOSEFUL POWER

Are you where you belong?
Are you living the life you want to live?

For if you are not,
if you are harboring excuses
if you are taking the potholed easy street
if darkness has shrouded you like
a suffocating blanket of mighty weight,

then roll steady my friend,
for we've all been there.

You must remember the deep strength
within soul.

We have power to lift stone,
purposeful power to place ourselves where
we belong.

I MUST SAY

With people trying to kill me,
with an assassination attempt
unsuccessful,
(almost a backwards compliment)
knowing they will return
and try again,

I must speak, for
if they were to kill me tonight,
these words I must say:

Be kind and patient with one another
Communication is so severely important
Listen truly
Love one another the way
They want to be loved
If anger rises within
Walk into the woods and let it out alone
Never destroy our planet
Defend her fervently
Be with family and cherish them deeply
Never consume another with your darkness
You have the strength within to find light
Give everything you are to the world
Strive to be Christ-like
Find who you are and blossom
You were meant to be you.

THE GREAT WAVE

A new fire has lit within my soul
once again, surge of joy and
emboldened physiological energy
upon each holy occasion.

Like a great wave each surfer
dedicatedly waits for
I now ride not letting a drop of
inspiration become unevolved,
all is soaked and applied
as sponge mortar staircase to heaven,
arising within new light,
chasing and catching
each dandelion seed in the wind

for I am soil I am rain I am
Golden Eagle flying in the sky.

SOMEWHERE

Finding a place to sleep at night
isn't always easy,
for the mountain grade and thick
underbrush
yields rare spot.

In the ink of night, it becomes two options,
hike on
until a sleeping crevasse is discovered
or create one,

as a lion in the trees
or burrows of wolverines,
tuck into furrow of Mother Earth.

Smile softly at bears as they sniff forehead.

Whisper tree's heavenly lullaby.

Gray owl hooting ply,
full moon,
eye,
you,
somewhere.

SO VERY B.C.

I could throw few things into a bag
Order a Lyft
Be at the airport
In 49 minutes
Choose a flight
To somewhere I've never been
Soar away unencumbered

But it is not quite time
For that again
For there
Is much to be done
Here at home

STILL HEALING

Some nights

Are much more difficult than others

Unable

To keep myself together

Unable

To believe I am whole

Shattered

Into the pieces I have stitched and picked

Together and apart again

I am still healing

OBLITERATION

The sun bores into me
The way I wish she'd look at me

I open my mind, my mouth,
My soul, I let it enrapture my whole

All of time coalesces into now
In this adoration that rescues

In this nirvanic trance
One with each vibrating molecule

A beat in the cosmic
Deific ripples of eternity

Although I know,
Too much of this love

Too much of, take my all,
Shall be my obliteration

IN BED

My heartbeat is in bed somehow home,

naked between blankets feeling bittersweet,

having convinced demons to take the night off.

Alone I laugh, slithering smoke into

the one-bathroom light seeping across

sleepy bedroom, as a moor may sing

when it is sad, as I sing tonight,

my heartbeat in bed.

CHANGE SHALL BLOW THRU

Each season
Begins and ends
With a dynamic tempest

Each storm
Always wears
One final stentorian blast

To make room
For peace to fill
All space

To harken soul
The liberating truth
Of light

A RIPPLE

One seed one tree

10,000 more

One flame a fire

Thirsty for all

One human a ripple

That can save this world

ANCHOR

I was doing so well

We hadn't talked for many weeks

And then you reached out
And said a little something

Sunk me
Back
Into the depths
Once again

Your word
An anchor
Around my neck

MUST LET GO

She wanted me to heal
Too quickly
As if thinking the gash
Much less than it is

She wanted to be friends
Calm second place
To everything we'd built
And bled

I cannot do either
It is far too soon,
And so now it seems
We are nothing

Perhaps we share a moon
But even then
That is me holding on,
I must let go

MY WORDS

Hanging out on a Friday night
At the place they tried to murder me

Same day
5 weeks later

With eyes on all sides
Completely aware

Come at me
Try to eliminate me again

I cannot die
For I have written my words

And yet

So many books I've still to write
So much world I must help save

MAP

Music

Meditation

Adventure

Patience

Prayer

Intention

Love

Nirvana is within

Distinguish fire upon tongue

COOL OFF

alright
wild heart on fire
it is time
to cool off a bit

wounds
never mend if
I keep ripping
them open again

Breath

Refocus

Believe

INFINITE TREASURE

I go to bed feeling full
After spending
A powerful beautiful day
With friends
Who have become family

Infinite treasure
This is
Knowing all of you

VAULT WITHIN

There is a vault buried deep within my soul
Where oracles brew
Mystic knowledge
Desires
Pushmi-Pullyu passions from other worlds
Stored away with purpose
Only to be liberated
Whence angels and demons
Have seduced élan-vital's objective.

Within this vault
Morality and immorality pace in shapes
Battle and embrace
Torn within prison of pandemonium
Disciplined as a hammer's strike,
Eternal verdict
'til time beyond this inhumed vault
Voraciously howls its ethereal demands.

AWAKE AGAIN

The wild within me stirs
Out of hibernation
Waking wobbling striding
Lava spitting over brim

Like the pioneers rise
Each mountain day
Making love
Where bears did

Eyeing horizons
Occult of knowledge
Heartbeat fury gnash
Into the dawn awake again

GRACEFULLY FORWARD

Whatever has been, has been.
Whatever happened cannot be changed,
There is no rewinding, there is only
Our response, how we move forward.

Character is determined in such a crux,
Ego perhaps seeking revenge upon past
Which only exasperates, injures, prolongs;
We must live with poise and forgiveness,

With others, with our own self.
Strength found in control,
Wisdom in calm decision,
Peace a meditative choice.

BATTLE OF BRAYS

The universe is mashing into itself
as if orcas are fighting grizzlies,
as if assassins are eliminating tyrants,
and yet,
none of that is,
palm drip honey slap of peace eliminated,
gregarious predicament of morality.
Feasting upon moral all concave,
sheep willing to die for other sheep,
slaughter the onslaught of silence,
or at very least shouting into the wind.
Piss on me,
into my mouth,
let me taste something finally true,
and when you are finished
I will not kill you,
I will ask why you obeyed.
Cry cry cry!
Bray you beast of society!
Bellow your recipe of despair,
glow upon the wall so we can all see it all
for no more it must ever be.

AS I

I will lay
Miserably happy
I will stand

As a sloth
Or
As a hungry lion

I shall pursue
All that my soul has
Declared I must

True eternal power
God
Is in me

I shall live
As I was born
And as I shall die

TEMPEST

The storm was here before it arrived
Announcing itself
By change of scent in the air
By the way she wore her hair
With new ripples of energy
That only spines can hear
Tricking all time
Into a look over shoulder
Concocting change
Creating waves
Tempest with invisible ardent fingers
Scratching all parallels into one
Shedding skins into memory
Shaking the universe
Upon the brink of precipice
Pressed up against chasm
Infinity advancing ferociously
Gnash of fate versus decision

I AND YOU

Despite any tragedy
Any horror any evil,
No matter
The pandemonium of existence

We bond together,
We fight for good
As a community.

We dispel negativity
And replace it
With positive actions.

We instill trust within each other
Through communication
And honesty.

All of us will hurt.
We must face the dark alone,
And yet when you open your eyes,
When you are ready,

I and you
Shall always be there
For each other.

ASH OF ONCE WAS

He asked me for a lighter

Slide across fold-up table

He pulled out crumpled bills

Then lit them aflame

"there is nothing left,
what does money matter…"

Oculars dark satanic success

Beyond the blaze

Deeper than the hurricane

Ash of once was

Dripping beyond

A well we can fathom

A CALL TO ARMS

Despite it all,
we have a giant opportunity
directly in front of us.
The action must be now.
Looking us in the eye the universe
poignantly questions,
how shall you respond?
Will you grow as a community
or scatter into chaos as imbeciles?
Sheep falling to death in hordes off a cliff
or calm focused gathered strength
with intentional purpose.
Masses have always been fickle,
running amuck when mayhem strikes,
lured by the tune of a selfish piper
and also, at times
creating an army of civil force
that demands and attains
powerful necessary change.
What an immature shame the former is,
when each of us
one by one together
can build a chain of focused warriors,
fighting
for an evolved healthy vibrant
beautifully balanced life.

It is not time to mock,
it is not time to live in fear,
it is not time to selfishly discard truth,
it is time to grasp the reality of
transformation,
to understand the planet is angry,
to fathom that this is our fault.
It is time for humility,
we must shed our pride,
we must rise above history.
It is time for a solidarity this world
has yet achieved.
You and I, now.

ST. PATRICK'S DAY

Empty bars
Empty streets
Empty aisles

March 17
Everyone in quarantine
No glass shattered floors
No DUIs
Nobody kissing on sidewalks tonight

Listening to the eerie silence
No holiday surrenders
Sipping dark patio wine
Staring into dim dynamic stars

A lone bagpipe begins to sing
Far away like a candle
Unobstructed by no other sound
Irish lullaby's drift thru town

Tune of misty midnight moor
Whispering tenderly
Upon any of hope's closed doors

Alone or not
Perhaps some of both
The night returns to silence

OH DARLIN

Tonight
I am suffocating the urge to call my east
coast family.
I have woken grandmother too many times,
before she could even make coffee,
my end of day her start of day,
funny how it meshes like that.
Some years ago, after Grandfather passed,
I went to Georgia to be with her 3 weeks.
Out there on the GA-FL line
big bright porch facing cattle and acreage
dirt road and pine-sharp horizon
much work to be done,
pecan trees scattered about
in social distance,
wine bottles
chocolate chip cookies
pain from past
spilling into Grandma's kitchen.
So, after I finished the fence for the day,
we went on an adventure
in search of a guitar,
west and east,
pawnshops almost to Savannah,
a country girl's eyes shined,
few good-ol-boys wanted to scalp me
and my long hair,

but then in Blackshear
tarnished in a dusty corner,
we found the instrument.

Home to country Georgia porch we drove,
to heat up some ham and banana pudding,
watch the sunset,
strum and hum.

FRESHLY SHAVED

I wish you could
Touch my face
With your fingers
And your lips

I miss the warmth
Of another
A gentle love
Essential

Yet in these lonely
Patient days
Much like a
Lady slipper

In the forest
Life unseen
Own love within
I remember

THE BEGINNING

Watching the sun set
Soaking my eye with that
Descending orange sky
Seeing the mountains fade
Into blues crowned by
Gentle purple clouds
Listening to the silence
Of birds nestling into nest
As if there was no virus
As if the earth is at peace,

I know this is not true
And yet, for the birds it may be.

CORONAVIRUS VIEW

There is a chickadee outside my window,
I wonder what it deems,
Of all the cars and all the humans
Scattered from their seams.

Tilting head side to side,
Staring into no airplane blue,
Little branch hopping chickadee
Enjoying peace of something new.

HEAT OF TIME

Cannot kill this with a gun
Cannot sleep until it's done,
Satan must have climbed some stairs
Seeking Job once again.

A worthy life I have lived
Says the father to his son,
Serpent head of seven seals
Steals breath of could have been.

Watch the water as it falls
Once at peace now released,
Into aeon unresolved
Beneath the heat of time.

THIS TOO SHALL PASS

I have much hope yes
But I also feel much melancholy

Most nights of late
I have been able to set the latter aside

But tonight
Unable to sleep

As I ignore the pain in my body
I cannot detach from the pain in my soul

AN UNEXPECTED GIFT

A strange turn of events
that I would never have expected

But as I battle this virus

As I lay here
Sit there
Breathe deeply aware

As I pray in a way
I never have before

As I seek knowledge and
Understanding amidst
All of the confusion and fear

I feel that I am actually
Finally
Healing
That the angry muddled past
Is fading away

And clarity
And peace is blossoming
Into who I am to be

YOU ARE STRONG

I wish that none of you would be infected with this virus. I wish that none of you would ever incur disease, heartbreak, pain; however, that is not how life is. There are many obstacles and trials, at times horrific, we each must face. And frankly, this you know, it is what allows us to understand joy. Without the hardships we could never achieve happiness.

When it is time for us to go through such a hardship, it is best to not try and divert or ignore or brush it under a rug, but to face it head on. Combat with fierce confident tenacity, intention to conquer the trail, be that however long it may. Reach into the arsenal you have created for yourself from past experience, wield the weapons you know.

PERSIST

The beast brawls
Ensuing surge of adrenaline
Or so it feels
Innate eternal embodiment

As ghosts are wind
As Polaris remains
As pink moon rises
With sliver asleep

So, anima persists
Within this tangible realm
Or beyond
Passionate beat of life pervading

DIVE INTO POSSIBILITY

I have summited
the mountain

A horizon
of vast opportunity
never before seen
lays before me

Now all I must do
is climb down
and dive into the interior
of possibility

STEADFAST BEACONS

So quiet
I hear frogs down by the river
An orchestra
Above hissing cackle of last flame

Owl screeches
For there are no tires on the road
Saturday night
Lovers in tangle or all alone

North Star
Holds steady within cosmic twirl
Steadfast beacons
Humble reminders from our world

I DREAM OF YOU

Each night within sleep's
Prison of dreams
I still search for you

I see you turn and walk away
Within faceless crowds

I fight to reach you
But each chimerical corner
Swallows your visage

Each morning I awake
More apt in stoic acceptance

Exhausted from battling
Willfully surrendering
To the mirage of what was

I breathe mindfully and rise
Grateful to be alive

A NEW ME

When heartbreak happens
after lava has cooled
gather all pieces
and build new armor
with the obsidious remnants

Unwilling to allow
that kind of heartbreak again
a new you has been forged
through fire
destruction the holy seed

When the past
knocks and asks
to be the mortar to your now
heart rearranged
stitched back together

I don't know yet

I am a new me

I AM ONLY HUMAN

I am the most human I can be.

Soaking up the dirt.

Remember me.

For the fact I chose to live wild,
For my poetry,
The music of me,
My desire to love and be loved.

It is you I long to inspire,
For you
To fully be all of yourself.

Let us seek until the end
Living unashamedly
Peeling away layers of heaven
Until we have either created it
Or dismantled its bones.

HAVE I?

Have I lived my life in such a way
that inspires others to reach for greater?
To be fully themselves,
to not side with the negative
but positively reach
into the deep possibility of beauty within?
Have I made you laugh?
Angry?
Uncomfortable with what you believe?
Have I shaken the canyons with honest howls
and trembled the mountains with my tender tears?
Have I made you analyze your very existence,
the power of you and what you can do?
Have I reached the core of our universe,
the soul of all of us?
Have I made this world kinder,
to each organism upon it and beyond it?
Has love penetrated as deep as it can?

If I have not,
then I still have much life left to live.
There is work to be done.

VOTE

As if everyone was listening
Even the dead
Rise up the spirit within us
Beyond us
All of us as the greatest mass
Of vibration
Destroying all negativity together
Revolting against
This evil empire, tearing down
Fascist tyranny.

For while they may govern us now
They can fall
All we must do is fight with unity.

BUSHWHACK THRU

We don't know
How it shall unfold

Bushwhack thru
Dense turmoil until

All of that
Is behind us

Gashed and bloody
Yet heart still beating

Belief revitalized
Love tenderly fervent

The coals of soul
Hotter than ever afore

NO JUSTICE NO PEACE

It has been a long time since the masses came together, all of us, for months, shut in and separated.

Yet for this, for the utmost importance of equality, we stand and shout and march shoulder to shoulder, chorus in solidarity for all black lives, to fight hatred, to be patient no longer.

Most of us masked, amidst the pandemic, battling in agreement, across the country in cities and towns, voices and footsteps and fists rise in unison.

Black Lives Matter.

We kneel with you, we listen and fight with you, there is no more time left on the despicable racist clock, no reason to be silent, to not fight against what must be destroyed.

No justice no peace.

No more police brutality, no more excuses.

A revolution of truth and love that shall be beaten back no longer is fervently afire.

I FIGHT FOR US ALL

When I was a runaway
Nothing could contain me
Just the wide heavy sky
And the honest breathing earth.
Being away from all those rules
Those fucked up greedy rules,
I was free, but
I was missing something.

I was missing you,
The fight in me
Is not only for me,
It is for us.

So, I returned as a zealous man,
To fight against those mongrels
Imposing their greedy immoral rules
So that we all may be free.

UMBRELLA IN THE RAIN

How incredibly cozy it is
To sit under a wide umbrella in the rain

Beneath this round shield
In my own dry cylinder haven
With a beer which tastes better with this
Sweater snug around my neck

And two eyes for all the colors
The rain seems to amplify

Like those dripping red flowers washed clean
And the orange road cones
With dirt descending like mascara
When she cried

All the verdant leaves dancing
With each rain drop splosh
And the pittering puddles growing larger
Each minute

I soak in the scent of the earth,
Filling my lungs with this natural cleanse

A FEW MOMENTS TO PRAY

I hike up the ridge and sit upon my favorite rock, facing east I look down upon the city.

From here I cannot feel the hatred.

Lights beneath stars appear soft and innocent.

Nestled cozy in the night I release to the wind and few moments of meditation.

I let myself mourn, pouring out tears I've held back, I shudder with the knowledge that this is reality.

Down there, in that civil twinkle is a land at moral war, there is an evil slithering which seeks to consume, and too within the bosom of the valley, a passionate army of love fights for equality and peace.

Why must humans hate? Why must the lights below be filled with dissension? Why must greed and ego blossom?

I shall sit here, lament until I am done, smoke a joint, pray, align my soul with the powerful beautiful truth of this universe, then hike back down into the battle and fight for love beside each of you warriors again.

LABYRINTH OF SELF

Seeking the deep inner truth of oneself
Is a practice marvelously terrifying

For doors are opened when knocked upon
Understanding is lost and in so gained

With safety of stagnancy tossed aside
The ride now rapines roaring thru caves

Depredated by your own decisions
Out of control one learns control anew

All imposing barriers abolished
Labyrinth of self now but passageways

Into a world of worth and freedom
Into the world of you knowing you

I BELIEVE IN YOU

In case, one last thing.

Be kind to everyone, not just humans, but all species,
Bugs - Aliens - Bears - Trees

Fight to abolish hatred,
The true heroes are those who stand
directly in the face
Of evil and say NO!

Forgive others and yourself,
For we are all maturing
And must learn to love beyond ego.

You were born to be you
And you are extraordinarily beautiful.

Seek the root of your soul,
Listen
Practice
Grow
Love to its purest possibility.

Stay wild
Don't let them tame you.

You'll figure out what that means.

www.ingramcontent.com/pod-product-compliance
Lightning Source LLC
Chambersburg PA
CBHW030430010526
44118CB00011B/573